Whole-Class Teaching

Minilessons and More

Janet Angelillo

HEINEMANN
Portsmouth, NH

Heinemann
361 Hanover Street
Portsmouth, NH 03801–3912
www.heinemann.com

Offices and agents throughout the world

Library of Congress Cataloging-in-Publication Data
Angelillo, Janet.
    Whole-class teaching: minilessons and more / Janet Angelillo
            p. cm.
    Includes bibliographical references and index.
    ISBN-13: 978-0-325-00971-1
    ISBN-10: 0-325-00971-6
    1. Effective teaching. 2. Classroom environment. 3. Teacher-student relationships.
    4. Interpersonal communication. I. Title.
    LB1025.3.A54   2008
        371.39—dc22   2007038775

Editor: Kate Montgomery
Production editor: Sonja S. Chapman
Cover design: Jenny Jensen Greenleaf
Cover photograph: © Superstock, Inc.
Compositor: Eric Rosenbloom, Kirby Mountain Composition
Manufacturing: Steve Bernier

Printed in the United States of America on acid-free paper
12   11   10   09   08   RRD   1   2   3   4   5

To Charles,
with love and trust

Contents

Acknowledgments

I am the sum of my experiences, all the books I've read, the conversations I've had, the places I've been, the people I've known. And it is these beautiful, generous people whom I thank for their care and help in writing this book, one way or another.

First, to fine teachers and administrators all over the country. You keep our work vibrant and alive in schools. It would fill an entire book to name you all, so I thank these few, asking the others to forgive me and know that I love and appreciate them all: Sarah Daunis, Rachel Moramarco, Paul Crivelli, Lisbeth Arce, Kerry Sullivan, Kathy Lauterbach, Lucretia Pannozza, Shari Robinson, Janet Katz, Gene Solomon, Israel Soto, Irma Marzan, Sharon Meade, Leonie Hibbert.

Of course, I cannot write a word or teach a lesson without remembering all that Lucy Calkins has taught me. Her brilliant and seminal work at the Teachers College Reading and Writing Project changed my teaching life and its trajectory. I thank her for all her work on behalf of literacy and teachers everywhere. Lucy, thanks for believing in me.

My dear colleagues and friends—Isoke Nia, Carl Anderson, Leah Mermelstein, Shirley McPhillips, Gaby Layden, Laura Robb, Ralph Fletcher, Ruth Culham, Lester Laminack, Katie Ray, Katherine Bomer, Jeff Anderson, Lola Schaefer, Linda Rief, Jim Blasingame, Aimee Buchner, Frankie Sibberson—your thinking is with me always as I teach and write.

I thank those who have supported me in hundreds of quiet, loving ways: Carol Bogen, Avis Sri-Jayantha, Meredith Downey, Mary Attanasio, Kay Rice, Janet Hough, Susan Goodman, Martha Holden, Hugh and Sirka Barbour, Jane Berger, Barbara Rutledge, Karen Holtslag. To my spiritual director, Gaynell Cronin, I give thanks and blessings, along with Nan

Weir, Patience Robbins, Father Mike Duggan, and Carmela DiNobile. May you all be blessed on your paths.

I thank my wise editor, Kate Montgomery, for her patience and insight. Thank you for knowing the words to say and the words to hold back. Thank you for thinking with me to make me smarter. Thank you for holding my hand through the valleys. You are friend and confidante, teacher, and muse.

I thank my sister, Marina, for her love and friendship, and my delicious nieces Kate, Mary, and Lisa. Thanks for showing me how to have fun and be "cool"—OK, sometimes.

Of course, I've saved the best for last. Charles, Mark, Cheryl, Alex . . . come, my loves. It is time to laugh and play and celebrate. Let's eat!

Introduction

My mother was a chocoholic. She dribbled chocolate syrup into her coffee long before "coffee boutiques" were on the planet. She squirreled away pennies to treat herself to chocolate ice cream once a week. She asked for brownies for her birthday and counted the days until Valentine's Day brought an entire cardboard heart filled with gooey delights. Any chocolate, anytime. She was not a thoughtful, selective chocolate eater—she loved it all. She ate chocolate the way her mother did, and her grandmother before her—with abandon, delight, and some degree of guilt.

But all chocolate is not created equal.

Although I have inherited the great chocolate sweet tooth, I have discovered—through, ahem, careful sampling, serious research, and hours of grueling investigation—that there is some chocolate that gives me ecstatic satisfaction, and other chocolate that falls flat. Chocolate syrup from the supermarket just isn't worth the calories it costs, no more than the Halloween packages of small-bite chocolates can satisfy deep longings. But dark chocolate from France, hazelnut dotted chocolate crèmes from Italy . . . these are the chocolates for which I wait and work. I have expensive taste. I want chocolate that is an elegant work of art. Chocolate I can dream of and live off for a long, long time. Chocolate that is significant, not supermarket ordinary.

Just like teaching.

The process of teaching deserves to be an elegant work of art. It requires lessons that students will muse over and live off for a long, long time. And instruction that is significant and wise, not ordinary and common. Students deserve teaching that is the finest chocolate for their learning cravings, teaching that creates yearning and living for learning. Teaching must be—forgive me—Belgian chocolate for their learning souls.

We all know that teaching is an active, mind-expansive, and transforming profession. It is active in body, mind, and spirit, for few teachers ever can sit still; it is mind expanding in the hundreds of pedagogical and social decisions the teacher makes every day; it is transforming, as deep, constant, and thoughtful interaction with other humans usually is. It strengthens teachers' thinking and their souls, and at its best, it engages teachers in the process of cocreating knowledge with students and figuring out how to help students learn. Linda Flower (1994, 3) tells us, "Teaching is a theory-building enterprise. That is, it is a hypothesis-creating, prediction-testing process that leads to the framing and reframing of action. Theory building is an act by which teachers construct an imagined frame for actual pedagogy." It seems then, that good teachers create hypotheses every day for what their students need in order to understand, and that based on observation of student performance, good teachers are willing to reframe or revise their own work.

Good teaching is elegant; it is artful. Like good chocolate, it is rich. It consists of clarity, revision, assessment, and thorough planning. In essence, it is instruction that models what we want students to do in their learning lives. In reading and writing classrooms, good teaching demonstrates the literate life and literate mind in their complexities and beauty.

Fortunately, many recent teacher educators have researched and written about the benefits of small-group and individual instruction. Small-group instruction in reading, and to some extent writing, is now considered essential for a healthy instructional program. (Fountas and Pinnell 1996; Calkins 2000; Tomlinson 1999). In addition, most teachers now understand that individual teaching, also know as *conferring*, is where some of the most powerful teaching can take place (Anderson 2000; Calkins, Hartman, and White 2005). One-to-one conferring provides time for teachers to study each student's needs and to design individual teaching to support his or her learning. In the best classrooms, teachers work hard to balance small-group and individual instruction to scaffold students' growth as readers and writers.

But what about whole-group instruction? To what extent do we examine established and traditional teaching practices and reflect upon revising our teaching work? How can our whole-class teaching reach the maximum number of students—with all their varied learning styles and interests— with one brilliantly rehearsed and precise performance per content area per day? In what ways have we pushed beyond well-known and respected formulas (Hunter 1969) to gather the minds of our students together in unity and clarity of understanding? How do we understand the literate learning community as the foundation for learning (Peterson 1992)? And how have standards movements and high-stakes testing impacted not only the content of teaching but our methods as well?

In many ways, whole-class instruction is one part of teaching that has not been examined, because so many of us believe we already know how to teach. Small-group and individual instruction are new, so we sense the urgency to study them, but whole-class teaching is, in one form or another, centuries old. How do we revise something we've done much the same way for so long? It is often said that many teachers teach the way they were taught or the way they perceived teaching when they were students. Could this lead to sloppy teaching that is rambling, unfocused, or centered on activities rather than building true knowledge? How much teaching is merely assigning or quizzing? And to what extent have we moved forward with technology and cultural change? When we consider that many students come to school with new ways of knowing, such as computer and video gaming skills (Gee 2004; Shaffer et al. 2005), how do we incorporate the changes of twenty-first-century life into our teaching methods?

It seems appropriate that we reconsider the medium of the whole-class lesson at this time. As modern life and the demands of education change exponentially around us, we must deliberately change our whole-class instruction to fit our audience, that is, the students who come to us with varying degrees of experiential knowledge and often with types of knowledge that exceed our own. The classroom of the 1950s or 1970s or even 1990s is outmoded. Life—and teaching—is different today. We now know more about "brain research" (Wolfe 2001; Jensen 2005) and about learning styles (Silver, Strong, and Perini 2000). We know more about making thinking visible as a way to teach, and about "habits of mind" (Perkins, Costa, and Kallick 2000; Sizer 1992; Meier 1995; Costa and Kallick 2000) we want to model for students. We've gone beyond teaching as information dumping to focusing on cognitive skills and processes. We understand paradigm shifts from "I taught it, but *they* didn't get it," to "I taught this, but my teaching was not effective enough." We recognize the changing culture that affects the lives of our students, and we know we never can go back to the factory schools. The factories are gone, and factory teaching model isn't relevant anymore.

In this book, I will not attempt to pull the rug out from under long-standing good teaching practices, though I am not shy about examining methods and activities for those that have purpose and those that don't. To paraphrase Socrates, the unexamined teaching life is not worth living. I believe that in the face of ever-increasing governmental and societal demands on the efficacy and efficiency of education, we must stop and examine best whole-class instruction practices carefully. We are asked to accomplish more every day. Yet, as Lucy Calkins says, "Time is all we have." We must use it wisely. There isn't a minute to waste in outmoded or ineffective practice. We must move into the twenty-first century with speed.

Certainly teaching is a cyclical process (Tyler 1949), which contains re-planning, redevelopment, and reappraisal. This book will look at this cyclical nature of teaching and apply it to whole-class teaching. Others have examined the concept of short and precise teaching in the form of minilessons (Calkins and others); we'll add to that examining the minilesson as an art form, and how its seamless beauty is a vehicle for sharing content information and growing new thinking. We'll also look at other forms of whole-class teaching, such as share sessions, and times when minilessons look different from the usual form. Ultimately my purpose in this book is to raise our understanding and practice of whole-class teaching to the level of art. My hope is that you will understand what a gorgeous minilesson feels like and will have the confidence to know you can write and execute exquisite minilessons yourself.

I have arranged this book in two sections. The first section will look at the power of teacher modeling as a way of life; that is, the implicit ways we teach students to live as learners and compassionate humans through our whole-class instruction. Active, mind-expansive and transformative teaching can only happen when teachers dedicate themselves to the art of teaching, to study of students' needs, to professional self-examination, and to curricular interpretation and innovation.

The practice of teaching is the second section, focusing on decon-structing the minilesson itself and on curriculum planning, self-study, and rehearsal. Content, standards, and assessment are the ingredients of fine teaching, but the information itself is only the beginning of good teaching. Finally, I reflect on the paradox of teaching: good teaching appears simple, yet is quite complex. Most great artists, actors, musicians, athletes, chefs, and so on make the difficult appear simple. Great teachers do this too. It requires planning and focusing on methods, as well as a command-ing knowledge of content that allows for differentiation.

When I was a little girl, I fell in love with music. I've gone through jazz, rock, and reggae phases, and an addiction to everything Beatles. But one passion has endured through all my fickleness. This is my love affair with serious music—symphonies, concerti, oratorios, and all types of music that seem very highbrow. But the love, sorrow, anguish, and longing expressed in music is universal, if we would only listen. It's like teaching: great teaching is a window into the truths of humanity with all their sorrows, triumphs, and pains. The clarity and vision, passion and devotion of one fine teacher can carry us through our lives

I believe that watching great teaching is like listening to a magnificent symphony or sitting before a fine fresco. Like other masterpieces, well-executed teaching is a work of art. It comes from years of study and practice, a good amount of patience, intuition, and carefully honed talent. It requires the willingness to take risks, to put one's self on the line, and to sometimes pick one's self up after a failure. As practitioners of our art, we should be content with nothing less than stellar performances. There is nothing highbrow about it—it should be daily fare for all students.

Which brings us back to chocolate. When we investigate the vast field of fine chocolate, we attune ourselves to the chocolate of our own fancy: milk chocolate, white chocolate, coconut, raspberry, nut-covered chocolate. Personally, I wouldn't walk a mile for a candy bar, but I'd fly an ocean for *chocolat noir*. I prefer chocolate that is *art*, made from recipes decades old and carefully fashioned into shapes to delight and sooth my fancies. Like our tastes for chocolate, we all have our teaching styles and our teaching personalities. I would never suggest that there is one way to teach or one chocolate for everyone. But by choosing only the richest, finest chocolate and the deepest, finest teaching, we set high standard for ourselves.

I hope this book will help to move our teaching from ordinary teaching, like common chocolate, to teaching that is exquisite, elegant, rich, and ultimately worth the time our students spend listening to us.

The Respectful Teaching Life

*Modeling Compassionate and
Intellectual Relationships*

Rain spatters the windows this dim October morning as I tiptoe into Rachel Moramarco's fourth-grade classroom. It's 8:40, and while Rachel sits in her rocking chair and reads aloud, students quietly unpack their book bags and hang their wet coats. Without pausing to sharpen pencils or chatter about homework, they hurry to sit close to her. They snuggle around her with expectancy, trusting that Rachel has something deep, exciting, and worthwhile to share with them.

Reading aloud is a daily ritual in Rachel's class, one that tells her students how much she loves literature and how much she respects them and their time as learners (Peterson 1992; Laminack and Wadsworth 2006a). Students know they are here to explore, to be comfortable, to be challenged, and to negotiate the cocreation of a dynamic and supportive intellectual community. The rain outside makes little difference to them—it is a fine day to gather together for learning.

As a visitor, I am struck by the sense of respect for each other that pervades the atmosphere. It shows in the exchanges between Rachel and her students and between students themselves. Mostly, there is respect, verging on quiet awe, for learning, knowledge, wisdom, inquiry and for the talents and struggles of each person in the room. I notice it in the kind way students treat each other; I hear it in the soft tones of their voices; I see it in Rachel's face. Even as she reads to the class, her eyes gaze over them. She nods to one with encouragement, she smiles to another with acceptance, she winks at one who scrambles in late. It is as if the eyes of her heart see each student with love and recognition.

So why does this matter? What difference does this make in Rachel's teaching, other than showing her kindness and teaching wisdom? How does genuinely living respectfully help students learn and love learning?

Those of us who choose to spend our lives shaping future generations have a unique and special charge. As the old saying goes, we "make a difference."

However, let us consider this: what difference do we make? Certainly we teach to help students meet or exceed standards, do well on statewide tests, and master a broad body of knowledge. But if that is all, then we can expect to be replaced by computers and online learning in a decade or so. To paraphrase Einstein, knowledge is not enough. We have higher work to do, work that cannot be taught by a computer program: the work of teaching truth and integrity, the work of loving learning, the work of modeling a respectful and respected life. Ultimately, we model how to honor ourselves, others, and the process of thinking itself. This is the greatest challenge of whole-class teaching.

Although teachers intuit that small-group and individual teaching must be tailored to children's needs, it is often a challenge to reflect those ideals while teaching everyone in the class. This is the grand work we do when we teach. Our facial expressions, our choice of responses, our body language and voice tone—every ingredient of demonstrating compassion and understanding are what students observe and emulate. This does not mean that we all must use the same tone of voice, or facial expressions, or phrases as we teach: on the contrary, I believe that we must be ourselves, with our individual personalities, our likes and dislikes, and our unique styles of teaching. But we must endeavor to become, through our teaching and work with youngsters, our wisest and highest selves, whatever that ultimately means for each of us. In the end, this results in teaching students *how to be in the world* no matter whom they are or where and when they gather with others.

In this chapter, I will examine several aspects of respectful whole-class teaching:

- inviting and expecting all students to learn

- choosing language and content to reflect respect and compassion

- modeling how to build supportive intellectual relationships

Inviting and Expecting All Students to Learn

Rachel Moramarco is not unique in her attitude toward her students. Many, if not most, teachers respect their students and hold their work in high esteem. They look beyond the seeming silliness of "administrivia," and they orchestrate classrooms that clearly recognize that their work is important. They live "above" it all.

However, some teachers become trapped in the daily struggle—they cannot extract themselves from the mountainous paperwork, or petty student bickering, or the weight of negative school culture. Life drags them down every day.

Rachel and teachers like her do not have a magical formula, nor do they teach in picture-perfect Norman Rockwell schools. What they have figured out is that their belief systems about students make a great deal of difference in their students' lives. Regardless of the students' attitudes toward learning, preparedness for school, home and family support, and so on, Rachel believes—knows—that most students want to learn. They want to be challenged and engaged. In fact, students who "act out" or "shut down" are often displaying an inner cry of "Teach me something! Please!" No one—especially children who depend on adults to design their learning lives—wants to spend days in boredom, conflict, or prisonlike lockdown. They all want to learn. Our job is to teach them.

When we examine our inner beliefs, often we must face an ugly reality: there are some students we are willing to let "slip by." "Things are fine when so-and-so is absent," or "He can't do anything," or "All she does is fool around" . . . these remarks say more about us and our beliefs than they do about the students. They are, after all, *children*. And as children, they have little control over their circumstances, their home lives, their medical care, whether a close relative is away at war, whether someone reads to them or loves them, whether their bellies are full, and so on. Most of all, they are not responsible if they are sent to school without a vision of loving learning and of how to "be" in school. It is our great privilege to teach them these things, no matter how hard that might seem.

Let's examine some beliefs teachers might have and look at how we might shift them around to create good. I know this takes practice, like learning anything new, but with time it will become a new way of thinking and reacting toward students. It will show all children that we respect them, no matter what, and we invite them to the great table of learning to feast with us.

Table 1–1 Changing Our View of Predictable Obstacles

Sample Beliefs to Be Revised	Beliefs with Compassion and Respect
My students are missing foundational knowledge.	Using small-group work and conferring, I will assess needs and build student skills.
My students come to school unprepared and with no respect for learning.	I'll make sure there are supplies available for them; I will model and show them how to focus and enjoy learning.
The curriculum is too difficult for my students.	I believe my students are capable of learning anything; I'll figure out how to teach it clearly and simply.
I have to spend too much time preparing my students for tests.	My very best teaching every day, along with deliberately making connections, will prepare students for all testing.
There aren't enough hours in the day to teach everything.	I can "watch myself" to notice when I get derailed—that is, how much time is wasted in power plays, routines, and nonteaching actions.

Certainly these are not all the beliefs—or obstacles—that make some teachers struggle. I think that struggle often happens from fear, frustration, and distress. We all know many things can potentially interfere with learning. However, the ideal is that no matter what the circumstances, we must not only believe that all children can and will learn, but that we can and will create the conditions for this to happen.

So here is how we respond to students when we expect all students to learn: we do not allow them to "wiggle out" of learning. We do not allow them to divert our attention. We do not allow them to fail at learning. We do not allow them to be content with shoddy work. We model and expect persistence, focus, and growth. Therefore, we offer them teaching that is fascinating, clear, simple, highly engaging, and filled with delight in the world, in learning, and in each other. We expect with all joy that they will come along with us on the journey. And we live with the belief that they can learn and we make them see it.

Table 1–2   Handling Problems with Professional Dignity and Respect for Students

Rules for Respectful Teaching	Why and How
Maintain composure at all times.	Anger makes us appear out of control and undignified; when anger threatens, speak very softly or not at all; controlled anger is appropriate in certain cases, such as when a child bullies another; intervene in disruptive situations with professional displeasure.
Keep teaching no matter what happens.	Keep supplies ready. Establish humane bathroom routines. Hold close to you the child who drifts off. Ask the office not to page you unless it is an emergency or only at certain times; begin again after interruptions; let all staff know your teaching schedule and do not welcome visits or interruptions. (Of course, you would stop teaching if a student was hurt or crying or bullying another, but that is using common sense.)
Quietly welcome students who are late. Just smile, or say something like, "Oh, we're so glad you are here. We have some wonderful things to talk about with you."	Avoid tenseness and embarrassment for student; let student quickly join the group.
Assess reasons why and make adjustments for students who do not work; teach students that we all work in school.	Recognize that not all students learn at the same pace. Provide opportunity for students to have choice, to move around, to work in groups, to create alternative products, to write on a computer.
Avoid confrontation that may end in a power play or substantial wasting of time.	Allow no opportunity for students to postpone instruction by "pushing our buttons"; like us, students do not want to lose face, so just move on even if the line isn't straight, all eyes aren't on you, or the pencils aren't sharpened, and so on.

Choosing Language and Content
to Reflect Respect and Compassion

Often teachers feel that they have little say on what to teach, but in most cases, things are not as rigid as they appear. Even if you teach from an anthology or a districtwide unit of study outline, or you have been given scripts to follow, let's still assume that you have some choice. Where? Within any "program," there is great opportunity for teacher—and student—choice. You just need to know where to look.

Every day we choose words in casual conversation and instruction that impact student lives. Peter Johnston tells us in *Choice Words* (2004, 9), that "Language . . . creates realities and invites identities." The words we use can invite or forbid, welcome or deny, clarify or befuddle. They can teach students to view themselves as high achievers and to have high expectations in personal learning. Often, we are using words that our teachers used with us, rather than considering how we might use language more effectively with students.

Let me emphasize that I am not advocating we all use the same words or phrases for teaching. That would reveal a lack of respect for *teachers* and for their work. But I do think it is wise to "listen to ourselves" regularly to assess how our words convey our feelings to students. What words do we use with students we like? With students who try our patience? When we are tired? When we are explaining something for the third time? How do we demonstrate our professionalism by our choice of words? Our love and respect for our work? Our respect for ourselves as teachers and thinkers? Somehow I cannot imagine my lawyer entering the room yelling, "Listen up, you guys!" or my doctor telling me she is sick and tired of my nonsense, even if she is. Their professionalism keeps them from using certain language no matter what they are thinking.

Let's read a partial transcript of a minilesson by a sixth-grade teacher and notice the ways her choice of language indicates respect for learners and learning. Her teaching point is that the first step of interpretation and eventual writing about literature is reading and discussion. Knowing what to discuss can come from recalling previous knowledge.

Transcript of a Poetry Minilesson, Grade 6

Teacher: Readers, let's meet together in the teaching corner. We'll begin in two minutes. Please sit with your partners. *[Teacher sets timer and goes to cor-*

ner to wait. In a conversational and soft voice she begins.] Yesterday we spent some time talking about and listing on the chart what we know already about poetry. *[Teacher points to chart.]* We mentioned some favorite poets, some poems you've read, and the original poetry books you wrote back in fourth grade. So we agree that reading and writing poetry is not brand new to us. Today I want to talk to you about another dimension of poetry study: it is that knowing how to talk about poetry is a way to prepare for writing *about* poetry. *[Teacher places "Ode to My Socks" by Pablo Neruda on overhead. Teacher reads and thinks aloud about the poem. Then she rereads and jots some notes in margins to prepare for discussion with a partner. What she wants to discuss refers to earlier teaching (for example, theme, personal response, connection to the world; i.e., something the class knows already).]*

[guided practice] Let's practice what I've just showed you. Read "Ode to My Socks" again and look for something we've already studied that you could talk about with your partner. You can refer to the chart of previous reading minilesson lessons to get ideas, perhaps from our read-aloud books. Then turn and talk with your partner. *[Teacher listens to conversations and takes notes to prepare processing.]*

[processing] Thinkers, let's come back together. I heard one partnership talking about how Neruda takes such delight in the socks and how that honors his friendship with Maru Mori. These partners said that they could read poems looking for themes that we've noticed in other books we've read, such as the theme of friendship. *[Teacher writes "Theme of Friendship" on white board.]* From listening to their conversation, I think I would add that we could notice what poets write about and how they make small things seem very important. *[adds "Make small things important" to chart]* I heard another partnership talk about how what Neruda wrote was surprising, because he saw ordinary socks in a different way. So another way to read poetry is "Look for surprise." *[writes on white board]* So when we reread the three things on our chart—theme of friendship, make small things important, look for surprise—we see that when you read poetry, you don't have to worry about what to talk about. You already know so many things about what to notice as you read books, and you can use those ideas to help you talk—and eventually write—about poetry. Today when you read some poems, use this chart, and other charts around the room, to help get ideas for what you could discuss in any poem you read.

[charge to the class] So here is the work I want you to do today. On your tables are baskets of poetry books. I'd like you to look through the selection and find one poem that intrigues you. Then read it several times, and try to use what you already know about how to read any text to help you notice something in the poem. Jot down what you notice, and be ready to talk with a partner about it in the last ten minutes of class. Now if you are ready to begin, please move quietly to your workplace. If you want more explanation, stay here with me for an instant replay.

What we can notice about this teacher's use of language to show respect for students and for learning

- She invites students to the teaching area and gives them a short period of time in which to prepare for the lesson, showing she values them and the brief but necessary time to reorient from one learning time to the next.

- She begins by recalling for students what they said in a previous lesson, showing that she respects their conversation.

- She refers to the previous lesson's information on a chart, showing that she cares enough to record their words.

- She is clear about what her intention is for the day's lesson; she writes it for them to read later.

- She addresses her students as "writers" and "thinkers," not "guys" or "kids." They are respected members of the community.

- She adds an item to the chart based on what she heard one partnership say, showing she is open to learn from her students.

- She keeps the pace going so there is little time for students to lose interest or get detoured.

- She does not bark her lesson, but speaks in a gentle, firm, self-assured voice.

- She invites all students to hear the "instant replay," avoiding stigmatizing students who don't understand the lesson immediately. She asks if they want another explanation, rather than if they need it, further minimizing stigmatizing anyone. Even in a risk-free learning community, she is careful to choose appropriate language.

What We Learn from This Teacher's Work

When we read this transcript, we see that this teacher is completely focused on teaching and on her students. She is not thinking about a parent meeting later, or a phone call she must make, or when she will get to grade all those papers, or even the student who may try to derail her lesson (he's sitting right next to her by design). She is completely *there.* So one important point we learn from her is to completely focus in the moment, to live in the "now" of that lesson, and therefore to be flexible and honest about teaching. No doubt, her students intuit her complete attention and her devotion and careful planning of the lesson.

We notice that she is extremely well prepared, showing students her attitude of thoughtfulness and seriousness about the work they do together. She weaves back and forth between past lessons and the current one, showing them that all lessons matter. When I asked her about this, she answered that she wants students to feel that missing a day of school is missing a great event, which of course it is.

We notice that she mingles with her students, quickly assessing how they are managing in their learning, and using what they say or do to plan her next steps. She is confident and comfortable, flexible and on her toes, yet single-minded in knowing this lesson is an important step in the chain of lessons she will teach.

Finally, we sense her deep respect for her students. She values what they already know and has confidence in their ability to learn whatever she decides to teach them. She knows she may have to differentiate for some learners but also knows they will all, at some point, get it. No child is left behind—or held back from jumping forward.

I have gotten into a routine of taping myself at least twice a month— conferences, minilessons, meetings with colleagues, and so on. Then I listen to them, often in the car on the way home. I listen to the same tape with a different focus each time: How do I address others? How do I respond to questions? How to I choose words to clarify and invite? What do I need to work on? Is my hilarious New York accent getting in the way of my teaching? Am I validating students' colloquial language while holding myself to a professional standard? How can I revise and make my teaching better? I suggest that you try this also. You will have different questions to ask yourself, but the purpose will be the same: recognizing that the way we use words will open up teaching to students or tragically stop their learning dead in its tracks.

Modeling How to Build Supportive Intellectual Relationships

Recently I went to a baby shower where I reconnected with colleagues from a school district in which I once worked. Most of the time we chatted about teaching, about how to support a struggling teacher, how to teach something new to a teacher who was fabulously smart, reconciling testing with instruction, and so on. The conversation flowed into what we all have come to love—intellectual stimulation and an exchange of ideas that helps us grow new and original ideas together. Frankly, I know these talks make me smarter. A few days later, a principal sent me an email, writing that she "so enjoyed talking about curriculum" with me again. Of course, I enjoyed it too.

Many students have not had the experience of supportive intellectual relationships, the way, for example, we may have with teaching colleagues or old friends, or other parents, or spiritual mentors, and so on. As adults, we move into these relationships because we enjoy the challenge and intellectual "fun work"; somehow time doesn't seem to matter when engaged in deep and fruitful conversation. When we help students develop these relationships, we lead them to another dimension of enjoyment and learning.

How can we do this? One way is to learn with another teacher (or coach or administrator) and model a conversation for students. Ask students to notice what you do as *thinkers* and *talkers*, rather than the content of the conversation. (You can record the conversation if you want to use the content later for teaching.) Here is a shortened transcript of a model conversation between two fourth-grade teachers, followed by the chart of what their students noticed about it.

Al and Laura teach fourth grade in an inner-city school. This is their model conversation about planning a literary essay unit of study. They brought their classes together in Al's classroom. Students were asked to notice how the talk pushed their thinking and what the teachers did to help themselves.

Al: Thanks for inviting me to talk about this, Laura. In fact, since I got your email, I've been looking forward to talking about the unit.

Laura: Me, too. I was trying so hard to figure this out, and I knew you'd be able to help me.

Al: Tell me what you are thinking so far, and then I'll let you know my thoughts.

Laura: Well, one thing is that I looked back over lessons on literary essay from last year, and I wasn't happy with most of them. I think they lacked the kind of energy I want in this study, and I think they didn't challenge my students enough. But I don't know what to do or how to start.

Al: That's interesting, because I felt the same way after looking over some old literary essay lessons. I said to myself, "So what?" as if my teaching wasn't deep or strong enough.

Laura: If you felt the same way, then maybe our teaching from last year wasn't strong enough. Maybe we've got some work to do to bring our lessons to a new level.

Al: But the classes did great work last year!

Laura: I know that, but maybe it was great work for *then*. We know more about writing now, so it's not great work for *now*.

Al: I see what you are getting at. *[long pause with obvious thinking and looking through papers]* So what should we do?

Laura: Well, we could do several things. We could examine some mentor texts to improve our essay bank of knowledge. Or we could examine student writing to decide which qualities of good writing we want to focus on in this unit and then plan from there.

Al: I also think it might help if we tried to write our own literary essays to see where it might be hard.

Laura: Ew, that sounds awful.

Al: Aha! You know that means that it's the thing we should do, don't you?

Laura: *[groans]* No way! I don't want to do that!

Al: Laura, it's probably just what we need. If we get into writing essays, and get *under* the thinking it takes to do them, we'll be able to figure out how to make our lessons better.

After the students complimented Laura on her honesty about not wanting to write, they then made the following observations, which Al wrote on a chart.

- Partners have something planned to talk about, like a problem, question, or some confusion; if possible, they let each other know in advance.

- Partners are willing to help each other by pushing to do hard things in order to grow.

- Partners listen to each other carefully.

- Partners are willing to do hard work together.

- Partners ask each other hard questions.

- Partners answer each other honestly.

- Partners have trust in each other's ability to offer good thinking and to help.

- Partners build a relationship over time.

- Partners look forward to their meetings and may plan regular meetings over time.

- Partners help each other dig under the surface to look for problems or for answers.

After the students completed the chart, Laura and Al decided that one focus for the unit would be to teach students to work together in the kinds of relationship they described above. Based on their observations of students, they had noticed the occasional adversarial relationships, the budding sense of competition, and flashes of disparaging pride for those who struggle. The intellectual relationship built on cocreating knowledge seemed more like the adult version of imaginative play—here we are together with a task and we are building it together, revising as we go along however suits us.

This model of play is significant. It made Al and Laura believe that students were already capable of providing intellectual support for each other, as they did in play. All they needed was to practice doing it with ideas. The two teachers planned out small-group work in which each person in the group brought a problem to the meeting and the others helped him or her solve it. Then the groups evaluated themselves on how well they did with helping find the solution. Firing questions at each other, saying "I don't know," and getting angry were not options. The groups had to discuss how thoughtful and adult they were in their discussions, referring back to the original chart they made from Laura and Al's conversation.

In the end, the students worked hard to become problem solvers. They still had work to do to raise the level of their conversation, but they began to build the self-confidence it takes to trust someone else with hard thinking.

Summary

We set the stage for learning in our classrooms each time we open our mouths to speak or cast a look in a child's direction or demonstrate our feelings with body language. As professionals, we must consider how language invites or forbids learning. Finely planned lessons must be accompanied by the teacher's focus, sense of self-control, and knowledge of using language to scaffold, support, clarify, and encourage. In the next chapter, we will look at validating students' experiences and using these to plan wise and effective instruction.

For teachers to do

- Audiotape a lesson or conference and play it back to recognize how you use language.

- Recognize your belief system about students and think about how it affects them for good or bad.

- Consider your intellectual relationships; how can other professionals help you become a better teacher? How can you help them?

- If you do not write, begin to keep a writer's notebook as a way to support your teaching and your insights into how to teach difficult ideas.

- Establish a practice that helps you live above everything with a singleness of purpose in your teaching.

2

Validating Students' Experiences

Wisdom and Integrity in Teaching

T he students in Sarah Daunis' fifth-grade class are writing nonfiction picture books for the third and fourth graders in their school. Sarah wants the students to be infused with her excitement for nonfiction, so she has given them broad freedom to choose their own topics. This has created some extra legwork for her. Nevertheless, she feels it is worth the time and effort. She tells me about one young writer who sent her several letters begging for resources to help him write about samurai. "I promise you that it is the thing I love best in the world!" he wrote. "How could I deny him the joy of writing about something he loves best?" she laughs, pulling out more books on samurai for him.

Together Sarah and I sit to plan the rest of the nonfiction picture book study. We discuss how the study must lift students' learning beyond the genre. We want them to reflect on themselves as they write. For example, we would like the student who loves samurai to think about why he's intrigued by them and in what ways he is like them. Clearly, he is not living in a past century, nor, we hope, collecting swords and knives; but their courage, strength, and loyalty are things that he might see reflected in his own life.

"I think my whole class can learn from this concept," Sarah concludes. "You can learn about yourself from studying about others."

I like to call this "searching for seeds of greatness." Wise and wonderful teachers like Sarah know that their best work happens when they search for and find the seeds of greatness in each student; eventually they follow this by helping students find those seeds of greatness inside themselves. Sarah uses language to show her respect for her students as humans and as learners, but she also uses every opportunity to open windows into the fine qualities she believes are inside her students. Sometimes this requires more nurture than at other times, but her belief in learners is always there. When we teach wisely, we believe, discover, and tend to the finest possibilities in all students.

In this chapter we will look at several ways wise whole-class teaching makes this happen:

- uncovering seeds of greatness in students . . . and in ourselves

- living into thoughtful silence

- modeling "turning around" thinking

Uncovering Seeds of Greatness in Students . . . and in Ourselves

I love to read biographies. Sometimes I read everything I can find on one person, and sometimes I read just one article or book and feel satisfied. In most cases, I like to consider the circumstances of the person's life and attempt to uncover what inside trait made him or her great—tenacity, compassion, courage, discernment, resolve, and so on. It amazes me that often I can find one trait that I have in common with the person, though sometimes I have to stretch a bit. With some reservation and humor, I could tell you ways that I am like (and unlike!) Beethoven, Jackie Robinson, Dorothy Day, Ella Fitzgerald, and Queen Elizabeth I, as well as ways I'm like a few notorious fellows from history. This musing on the inner traits of famous people has made me see myself in a whole new light—not caught in my insignificance and my shortcomings, but filled with hope, potential, and possibility. I have work to do to realize all my promise, but I also have courage to do it. Most of the time.

I believe this is a major reason for studying biography as a genre in reading and writing workshop. Reading about the lives of others should provide a window by which students begin to see the "seeds of greatness" in themselves. Which seeds of greatness were evident in the lives of these people when they were as young as our students? Which traits emerged later on, though no doubt they were waiting quietly to be revealed? Don't all student have some amount of nascent greatness inside them? Imagine students recognizing famous people, and themselves, as fine humans where seeds of greatness are born and grown.

Of course, these are only "seeds." After all, they are children. But with the proper care, seeds do sprout. Which of us as teachers would not delight in discovering in our classes the early greatness of a future Mother Teresa, Dr. Martin Luther King, Michelangelo, or Thomas Edison? We must see our students with eyes that look for greatness inside each of them. We have the responsibility to teach in ways that lead our students to recognize and develop their seeds of greatness.

The implications of this are vast. We no longer teach students who we think can't or won't learn. We no longer teach students who lag behind or who are "uncooperative." We no longer teach students who struggle or fail. They are all marvelous in our sight. We believe them into greatness because we know who they are and what they can become. Imagine facing a class filled with students who each have marvelous potential—it would have to change the way we speak to them and the way we teach. They are special, and they deserve special, that is, the best, teaching. It is a privilege to work with them, isn't it?

Let's look at this in the practical work of classroom teaching.

Ross is a fourth grader who rarely does homework, won't sit still, and dislikes reading and writing. His teacher confesses with guilt that she sighs with relief on days he is absent. She doesn't want to feel this way, but she is frustrated with his lack of commitment to work. As we observe him carefully during reading workshop one day, we notice he often bothers his nearby peers. When I talk to him about it, he says that he doesn't like the book he is reading, so he's curious about his peers' books. He also confesses that he likes to talk a lot! When we talk about the book he's reading, a picture biography of Michael Jordan, Ross says he's not like Jordan at all. Jordan is tall and athletic, but Ross is small. He likes fixing cars with his father and hopes to race cars someday. But when we make a list of Jordan's traits, including perseverance, strength, and talent, Ross seems happy. He says he has those traits too when he works with cars. He keeps going when he's figuring out what is wrong with a car, and he's strong enough to help his dad with much of the work. And he likes to talk a lot because he and his dad talk the whole time they are working—about the gears, their work, and cars they dream about. For Ross, talking is one way to get your work done. Soon he is beaming with the thrill of being like Jordan and believing that he can be a great success because of his "inside greatness."

In this case, the teacher and I focused on a student who lacked energy for schoolwork because he did not identify traits he had to succeed in, and out of, school. By helping the student "name" his inner "seeds of greatness," we help him begin to live into them. Furthermore, teachers can begin to explore each concept of greatness through discussion: What does *integrity* mean? How do you live with integrity? Who do we know who has integrity (historical figures and contemporaries)? How do you know you have integrity? And so on.

Essentially, the purpose of teaching a biography unit of study shifts: it makes a U-turn from studying the lives of famous personages back to the students. The teacher supports this by doing the following (See Figure 2–1):

- creating a chart listing "seeds of greatness" for the persons students are studying

- defining and explaining each trait or "seed"

- including an incident that shows this trait early in the person's life

- brainstorming ideas on how the trait helped the person succeed

- adding reflections on which traits we have and/or how we know and/or how we can develop them

Of course, this work need not be confined to biography study. It can be done in any study of characters, including fiction or a picture book study, as we saw at the beginning of the chapter. The main point is to turn students' focus in on themselves so they recognize their infant talents and infinite possibilities. As teachers, we must perceive and recognize these traits; we must teach our hearts into them.

Furthermore, our interactions with students might change dramatically if we, their teachers, believe they have seeds of greatness in them. In a whole-class setting, it would create a different way of presenting a lesson, reacting to students, listening to their responses, and scaffolding their learning. We would hear them differently—no longer searching for the "right answer," but waiting for pearls of wisdom under their young language and beginning thinking. And our teaching would have a new angle if we felt they were filled with great possibility and ability.

- We consider that each statement has hidden wisdom even if it is not readily apparent.

- We regard all members of the class as the brilliant beings of the future.

- We treat each student with respect by searching for seeds of greatness and naming possibilities for them.

- We trust that we do not know them well enough to make solid predictions about the future.

- We let them grow into their greatness gently.

- We let them fall and make mistakes; we don't expect perfection.

- We use their seeds of greatness to encourage them, not punish them.

- We trust that self-knowledge takes a long time.

One more thing: Don't teachers deserve to see the seeds of greatness in themselves? After all, we teach our best when we see ourselves as smart, compassionate, brave, insightful, wise, dedicated, persevering, or a host of other attributes. We must spend time musing on this and growing our confidence and pride in who we are as humans and as professionals. This musing leads to recognizing our greatness; our greatness increases our humanity; our humanity makes our teaching exquisite and brilliant.

Living into Thoughtful Silence

Several years ago, when Carl Anderson was the staff developer in my classroom, I recall a writing conference during which my student did not answer Carl's question. Carl just sat and sat, smiling, nodding, and waiting with patience and trust until she answered. I was a nervous wreck. I was biting the insides of my mouth! I wanted to shoot scores of suggestions at the student: What about this sentence? Did you try that? Show me your notes. Go back to your notebook entry. Where is your word list? And so on. But Carl sat there serenely watching her until she finally looked up and made a suggestion for revising her writing that was more insightful than anything I would have told her to do! Later when I asked how he managed the self-control to keep quiet, Carl told me that he had faith that students know much more than we give them credit for knowing. So he is willing to wait for them to reveal how smart they are. He is willing to listen.

Among the most important skills teachers must develop is the ability to listen. We listen all day to the many requests, arguments, and complaints of young people, as well as their answers to our questions and their efforts to put their thinking into words. As teachers, we must listen in deeper ways to what students are trying to say and what they tell us by what they mention or neglect to mention. Like actors preparing for their

Name of Famous Person	Seeds of Greatness	What We Think the Seeds Mean	How the Person Showed the Seed	Our Personal Life Reflections
Clara Barton	Compassion	To be able feel the pain of other people and be willing to help them	Worked on battlefields in the Civil War	
Madam C. J. Walker	Vision	To see that people need something and figure out how to fulfill it	Developed hair products for black women	
John F. Kennedy	Courage	To keep strong even when things look bad	Stayed strong even when his boat sank	
Derek Jeter	Leadership	To be able to calmly get people to trust and follow your example	Holds the Yankees together as the captain of the team	

Figure 2–1 *Class study chart for seeds of greatness*

roles, we must ask, What is the understory?—that is, what is going on underneath the words? This is the same kind of listening that doctors, clergy, and lawyers develop. What is the patient, parishioner, or client really saying? Teachers think: What is this student really trying to say? What kind of thinking is going on here? Is the student grappling with a concept, or merely grappling with the words to explain it? Sometimes it seems that listening is our most important work after all.

Name of Famous Person: Amelia Earhart		My Name: Carmella	
Seed of greatness	**What it means**	**Event from person's life**	**My life reflection**
Courage	Willing to do hard things even when dangerous	First woman to fly across ocean	I'm courageous: I go to visit Grandpa in the hospital even though I'm scared.
Curiosity	Wanted to see the world and see how far her plane could fly	Collected a team of people and planes to help her	I'm curious: I want to learn about more animals and I want to be a vet.
Individualism	Wouldn't stop her dream even though people thought she should	Made friends with Eleanor Roosevelt	No. Not yet.

Figure 2-2   *Student's personal seeds of greatness chart*

In listening, which is the stillness of refusing to supply an answer for a student or giving a student time to develop a thought or waiting that validates an unusual or unexpected perspective, we teach students that we respect their thinking and their thinking processes. How many of us really know how to listen? Are we comfortable with silence? Do we feel compelled to fill up every moment with chatter, even if we are doing all the talking? Why is this so?

Sitting with a student, permitting her to figure out something under a teacher's gentle care, is supportive and instructive. She learns that her thinking process is important. She learns that the struggle to figure out something is valued. She learns that teaching and learning are patient occupations. This completely differs from classrooms where silence is the rule because the teacher commands it, often because he is afraid of losing control or that students will veer off-topic. We must make silence a nonthreatening, comfortable place for youngsters. In this way, we will nourish depth of thought and support for it. It's a slow and quiet process.

In some spiritual disciplines, silence is highly valued as a condition for hearing and connecting with wisdom or divinity. Devotees of these practices spend time quietly in nature, in large rooms, in small cells—all attempting to train their minds to be still or to notice their thinking. Imagine if students were used to regularly sitting in quiet, not to practice wool-gathering or boredom but to learn to hear their own thoughts and to pay attention to how a thought matures in the mind. They would learn that the teacher does not jump in to supply all the answers but trusts them as thinkers. The teacher trusts that thinking will emerge from allowing thinkers to think!

Be assured I am not advocating guided meditation or any other particular form or practice of meditation. This would not be appropriate in schools. But we can borrow the concept for schools and adapt it for teaching. In our loud and noisy world, we can teach students to recognize and enjoy silence. The truth is that we all talk too much. We fill up the day with too many words. We teach students that we do all the smart or valued thinking in the room. And this is inexcusable.

Following are practices that we can use in whole-class teaching to demonstrate that thoughtful silence is—forgive me—golden.

- We wait for each other to finish speaking; we allow time for each person's thoughts to sit in the air before we go on.

- We do not fill in another person's thinking for him.

- We give each other the respect of wait time.

- We talk about our thinking and how it flowed from one place to another.

- We wait while someone struggles to find the right words or to revise her thinking.

- Sometimes someone suggests an idea and we just sit and enjoy thinking about it.

- We return to ideas to examine how our thinking has progressed.

- The teacher does little talking so that what he does say is valued as important.

- We listen to each other and to ourselves.

◈ We do not fear saying what we think or saying that we have more thinking to do before speaking.

Finally, I suggest you let students "see you think." Let them see the ways folks wrinkle their noses, frown, or close their eyes when they are thinking hard. What do you look like when you are thinking? (I look puzzled and dazed, often misunderstood by my teachers as zoning out!) Show them that you don't always answer instantly, that you consider your words before speaking, and that you weigh your answers carefully. Of course, you will also want to "think aloud," which many educators have taught us is invaluable (Ray 2000; Wilhelm 2001). Remember that before they even hear our words, they watch our bodies and our faces and learn a great deal from us about what we believe about them and about learning. Our whole-class teaching will be stronger if they know we teach from respect and wisdom.

Modeling "Turning Around" Thinking

I'm lunching with my niece Katie in a restaurant one winter afternoon. She must declare her college major in the upcoming semester, and she's lamenting how difficult it is to decide on one. I tell her that I still don't know what to major in—though thirty years ago I went with English and music, I could go back now and major in twelve other disciplines that fascinate me. There is enough to study for thirty lifetimes! She laughs and leans over. "So what you're saying, Aunt Jan, is that you can never make up your mind!" I sigh, guilty as charged, at least when it comes to what to read or study.

But I notice Katie's words: "So what you're saying is . . . ." This type of talking back to the speaker is very effective. Katie speaks back to me her distillation of what I say. In clear and bold language, she lets me hear the essence of my statement. She nudges me by asking for clarification and giving me a chance to rebut. She speaks the truth to me, rather than muttering to herself that I am acting ridiculous, silly, or just plain old. She is honest!

In whole-class teaching settings, we are honest with students when we listen thoughtfully to them and then ask for clarification. This helps students to reframe their thinking and decide if what they said is really what they meant to say. In a whole-class setting, we do well to help students understand that they must speak the truth with clarity; we also do well to let them hear how their words are interpreted by others. Teaching students to clarify statements by rephrasing and repeating them helps their thinking to become sharper and smarter.

Following are some examples of phrases teachers can use to elicit this rethinking.

- So what you're saying is . . .

- I think I hear you saying . . .

- Are you saying . . . ?

- Tell me what you mean by that . . .

- Tell me again what you are saying . . .

- So do you mean . . . ?

- Are you saying the same/opposite of what (name) said?

- When you said that, did you mean . . . ?

Restating students' words helps them to hear what they've said. Students certainly can say, "No, that's not what I meant," just as I could have told Katie that I am really quite decisive (not true!).

The trick here is to remain honest with students while scaffolding their thinking. In other words, Katie did not say a gross untruth. She drew a conclusion and stated what was in my mind already—she did not impose her thinking on me. We must be careful not to "put our words into students' mouths." We must be careful to walk the line of restating students' words in clear language without stealing their thoughts and making them our own or destroying their thoughts and replacing them with ours. In its worst extreme, a teacher might speak back something that was completely opposed to what the student meant, like Katie saying to me, "So you hated school." This would be a grave error and would teach the student not to respect his own thinking. Further, it is critical that we not be tempted to "lie" or fabricate what the student said. This would put words into a student's mouth that he didn't mean to be there. We want to scaffold and clarify, not twist the truth to get the answer we want. We are teaching students to clarify and qualify their statements, not just say what they think we want to hear.

If the previous warnings are heeded, this technique can be very successful. Let's look at some examples of how this works in a classroom (Figure 2–3).

This technique is also appropriate for students talking in small groups as well as discussion during whole-class instruction. Restating what someone else has said minimizes misunderstandings and confusion. In whole-class teaching, restating what the teacher has said helps students clarify and confirm the content of the lesson as well as the subsequent work they are going to do.

Student's Statement	Teacher Speaking It Back	What This Does
"I think the character in the book doesn't know whether to go with her dad or her mom."	"So I think you're saying that the character is confused about her feelings, right?"	Restates in broad terms that can apply to multiple texts
"I don't like the ending of this story."	"So do you mean that you think the author made a mistake with the ending?"	Ascertains whether this is a personal opinion or has evidence to support the statement
"I'm angry because there is just not enough information in this book."	"I think I hear you saying that you want to find more facts and you need other texts."	Validates the student's feelings
"I think that I can use my notebook to plan out my characters."	"Are you saying that you might make some charts and lists in your notebook to help you plan?"	Provides a label for what the student said
"My story stinks."	"Tell me again what doesn't work about your story."	Validate feelings while asking for specificity
"I don't understand what to do."	"So you mean that you need to hear the task again."	Offers words that student can use to ask for appropriate help

Figure 2–3 *Speaking back to students*

Summary

Before studying the details of whole-class instruction, it is important to lay a strong foundation of respect in the class. This includes listening thoroughly, valuing the thinking process, and gaining respect for the self by recognizing that greatness lies inside all of us.

Whole-class teaching is bigger than imparting information to a large group of students. It contains the information or content and also the skill of choosing words carefully for understanding and clarity and of nurturing young thinkers through the experience of thinking together to create knowledge. Once we establish (and reestablish) a supportive community, learn to use respectful language, and model that thinking and thinkers are valued, we can move to the next step of studying the practice of whole-class instruction.

For teachers to do

⟡ Ask a colleague to listen to your teaching and notice the words you use.

⟡ Practice speaking back or restating with a colleague.

⟡ Revisit your biography studies to consider adding "seeds of greatness."

⟡ Reflect on each student. What do you love about each one? How is each one special, talented, great? How do you communicate that to them?

⟡ Muse on your attitude toward silence, in and out of school. Write about it.

⟡ Consider how a love of silence can move you from a "teacher in control" to a facilitator of learning.

⟡ Think about yourself, professionally and personally. What are your seeds of greatness?

3

The Finer Points of Making Minilessons Work

Routines, Independence, Performance

Long ago, when I first began to teach, a colleague advised me not to smile until the winter holiday break. "If you smile, they'll think you're weak, and they'll take advantage of that," she said knowingly. When I was twenty and just out of college, her advice terrified me more than the first day of teaching (OK, the first year). Fortunately, today we laugh at such silliness, but that teacher was hinting—albeit in a weird way—at good advice. What she really meant was that teaching can only be effective if students know how to act in an academic environment. Rules, routines, and expectations make a classroom function smoothly (Peterson 1992). Although rules and expectations must respect students' humanity, including their physical and emotional needs, establishing them is necessary for instructional success.

In reading and writing workshop classrooms, where there is a surface appearance of complete freedom, routines for work are actually carefully planned and orchestrated. The quiet buzz and movement of work is what we might see in many working environments—a law office, a research lab, a hospital, a computer company. People have their work to do and are generally trusted to do it; those who can't or won't work are advised and helped to redirect their attention and energy appropriately. For the most part, people do their work as best they can. When teachers expect and believe the best from students, both the teachers and the students usually do their best.

What propels the workings of whole-class instruction is the strength of the understructure that is in place. This begins in the first minutes of the school year with the way the teacher greets students, models respect and expectations, and dives into the excitement of reading and writing immediately. It continues every day of the year: reteaching routines, gently reminding students of "how we act here," evaluating rules to revise them, including students in decision making, and teaching students to become independent learners and thinkers.

In this chapter we will look at several of the key elements that support our work. We certainly will smile the first day of school, and our smiles will contain the message, "This is a fine place to be and to learn: welcome. We'll learn a lot and we'll learn to be learners." But we will also study the elements that form the supports for clear and effective teaching. So let's examine the following.

- routines that support whole-class teaching

- student independence

- rehearsal and performance

- reteaching: always we begin again

Routines That Support Whole-Class Teaching

I like to get to school early so I can watch students enter the building and their classrooms. I learn so much about the culture of a school from the way students are greeted and how they greet each other and the teacher. When the teacher, principal, security guard, and office staff are waiting for students with smiles, it says they know this will be a good day.

I sit quietly in Rachel's room waiting for her to return with her fourth graders. She's been here early to prepare her work: her overhead projector is in position for her lesson, her read-aloud book is on the chalk ledge, the windows are opened, and classical music is softly playing. When they arrive, students joyfully spill into the room, unpacking book bags with efficiency, hanging coats and lunch bags in the closet, helping a student who is lagging behind. There is some chatter, but it's to remind each other what to do next. Without a word from Rachel, they collect pencils from a box and their readers' notebooks and quietly join her in the meeting area. The routine of beginning the day has gotten them from schoolyard to learning area in a few minutes—no whining, yelling, barking orders, or posturing. They are ready. And Rachel begins.

What I learn from Rachel is that a class with routines and expectations runs with dignity. These routines are not simply a matter of "handling" the class, or keeping order, as my long ago colleague suggested. These routines support Rachel's teaching. They give her the time and energy to teach. I watch and notice the following.

- The teacher immediately goes to the learning area ready to begin teaching; students have a sense of urgency about getting there, as if they might miss something important.

- There is no lag time before teaching starts and nothing gets in the way of starting the lesson; time matters.

- Students know where to put their belongings and do it quickly.

- Students know where to put notices and letters for the teacher to read later.

- Students help each other.

- They know where to get supplies, when to sharpen pencils, when to go to the class library, and so on.

- The teacher does not get distracted by details; it doesn't matter if someone is wearing his hat or forgets his notebook; without nagging, she begins to teach.

- Students are confident that there will be time for all their concerns to be heard, so no one jockeys for attention.

- Students know what to expect, so there is little repeat questioning. (I don't hear, "Do we need a pencil? Do we need our notebooks? Do we have to sit here?")

- A bathroom routine is in place (that is, no going out during the minilesson except for emergencies).

- The teacher's preparedness signals that this is important work.

- She begins just as the last student slips into place, as if she just can't wait to start.

This all seems so simple, but it is so important. In the course of the day, they are able to much work done. The routines help the class run smoothly and allow Rachel to teach. That is the point: routines allow us to teach (Table 3–1).

Table 3–1   Routines That Allow Teachers to Teach

Routine	How It Helps Teachers Teach
Transitions	Students know location of whole-class teaching area. Students practice and know to move swiftly from one place to the next. Students know where to sit in meeting area and expectations for sitting with partners, rotating seating arrangements, and so on.
Materials	Students know where to get supplies. Students know that missing supplies will not stop them from working. Students feel free to share or to borrow from teacher. Teacher is generous with sticky notes, pencils, and so on. Paper is available if notebooks are left at home.
What to bring to learning	Unless there is an announced change, students always bring notebook (or draft), pen/pencil, or book to minilesson. Teacher provides sticky notes in minilessons if and when needed. Students know where to sit and whom to sit beside. Students come expecting a lesson that is interesting and important.
Lateness	Student comes in quietly without shame or blame; teacher and others subtlety greet and welcome. Student drops bags and joins group. One student helps fill in information.
Bathroom breaks and drinking water	Students can go whenever nature calls, but not during minilesson (except emergency). Students can bring water bottles from home and can refill water.
Announcements, attendance, returning notices	Teacher has a basket for returning notices. One student takes attendance and teacher checks before submitting to office. Announcements are written on bulletin board/given at end of work time. Schedule for the day is posted.
Work rules	Students choose a spot where they feel comfortable working; they can stay there at end of minilesson. Students refer to chart of current and/or previous lessons to continue work.
What to do when students are finished	Students reread work; check the independence chart for suggestions.
Time	Teacher does not wait for all students to "appear" to be ready before she begins; no waiting for quiet or all heads in a row and so on; not a minute is wasted.

I write about routines with some trepidation. Routines take care of many of the daily details. They avert constant negotiation and decision making. They make us feel comfortable and at ease. However, there may be a tendency for some people to focus on the routines rather than what they are meant to accomplish. For example, it matters little if a student has a pen or a pencil, whether he has a hat on, or if he's going to the bathroom for the second time—what is the purpose of routines? Certainly it is not to argue with youngsters about them but to make the class run smoothly. A quiet whisper about too many bathroom visits is more effective than a major confrontation that interrupts the lesson, distracts students, and slows down teaching. Students learn just as well with hats on or off. The student playing with a hacky sack in his hand may just need to keep his hands busy to listen well, and this is not worth a confrontation. Students are quite smart—they will learn quickly if you can be deterred from your teaching mission, and some of them might enjoy distracting you!

Remembering that routines aid our teaching environment also means we'll want to reevaluate them from time to time. As students become accustomed to routines, you might ask their input on what changes they think would help move things along. Students are remarkably astute. I recall my students asking to move the learning area from one side of the room to the other so they could be nearer to the radiators. It had not occurred to me that they might be cold, but they were much happier in the new location.

Routines need to be taught and rehearsed. Rehearsing movement from one place to another is time well spent. Posting charts of routines that help us get our work done is also helpful. But if we return to the criterion for good teaching, this work is not worthy of a minilesson. So it must be taught at other times of the day, and we will discuss those in Chapter 6.

Student Independence

A young teacher I know was in tears one afternoon during dismissal. Her principal had come by to visit during the last period of the day and was not happy with what she saw. The teacher said to me, "I don't know what to do. They are only seven years old. If I don't spend the last period helping them pack up and buttoning their jackets, they will end up out in the cold with their book bags and their coats open." This poor teacher! She had not yet realized that the key to maximizing instructional time is to teach students to be independent. Within a month, her students were getting themselves ready quite nicely, and the teacher was thrilled to have gained last period for teaching. No doubt this is an extreme example, but it does illustrate how important student independence is.

Many times teachers ask how whole-class teaching could be effective and short. Once again, it is part of the woven fabric of excellent teaching. For example, there is little need for students who "get it" to sit through multiple examples; and for those who don't, it is less intimidating to work quietly with the teacher for support. When I suggest switching to whole-class teaching, here are some questions teachers ask, all of which are legitimate questions:

- What about students who finish quickly and don't know what to do next?

- What about students who don't get started working and fool around?

- How can I be sure they are really doing their work?

- How can I keep the class quiet enough to work?

- How can I expect them to work on their own without a teacher watching them?

- How can I turn my back?

- How can I keep track of what they are doing, especially if it differs from student to student?

- How can I know they'll "get it" in a short lesson?

Notice that many of these questions assume that the teacher's responsibility is to keep students in line. We have been conditioned to believe that we must keep students under control. However, imagine if students were engaged and independent enough that they had learning goals, knew what to do to reach them, assigned themselves independent projects and worked on them, and knew what to do when their projects were completed—all done without needing the teacher's constant monitoring. It would change the entire atmosphere of the room. The students would keep themselves in line, the way they do when they are engaged in play. It would be instructional heaven on earth.

Let's visit one classroom and I'll describe what I see. Paul Crivelli teaches fifth grade, and he has invested time teaching students to work without his oversight. I slip into a seat in the back of the room just as he completes his reading minilesson and sends students off to work. Students collect their independent reading books and notebooks and head to their reading spots—under Paul's desk, behind bookshelves, on the rug, at their desks, and on the sofa. They don't ask him many questions because his lesson has been clear and they know what to do next. One student signs out to go to the bathroom, and two go to the library to fill baggies with new book selections. Paul signals to a guided reading group and meets them at a semicircular table. As they settle in, the bathroom visitor returns—without delaying—and takes out his book baggie. Three students are writing in notebooks, and two are rereading the chart with the minilesson's purpose on it. A student with a question hands Paul a half-sized index card with a question mark on it. Paul raises five fingers to signal five minutes, and the student nods and sits to read until then. There is no anxiety in the room. Everyone is working and learning. Paul is maximizing every teaching moment.

How does he make this happen?

At the risk of stating the obvious, Paul is organized. His classroom is tidy (at least when students first arrive), and furniture and materials are thoughtfully laid out. He has collected all materials he needs for the minilesson in his teaching corner. Mostly, we have a strong sense that he knows what he is teaching and why.

However, beyond that, we have a sense of students knowing what to do even when Paul is not directing them. They have talked and rehearsed what to do when they are on their own. Their ideas are respected and scaffolded to make them meaningful and lasting. They know their work is not just to please their teacher, but to support their own learning and their choices. They know what to do and that their teacher trusts them to do it.

Figure 3–1 is a copy of the independence chart in Paul's room. Paul has explained that independence does not mean that students ignore what the teacher has asked them to do, but rather it helps them continue with meaningful work when the teacher cannot be there to suggest the next step. Independence does not take the place of following directions in whole-class teaching. It helps students trust themselves to carry on without the teacher's constant attention.

How does this look in sixth or eighth grade? In middle school, time is always a critical factor. Without a degree of independence, without loosening the reins to allow and trust students to act appropriately, teachers can find themselves battling with adolescent desire for independence all the time.

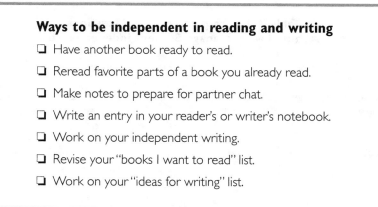

> **Ways to be independent in reading and writing**
> ❏ Have another book ready to read.
> ❏ Reread favorite parts of a book you already read.
> ❏ Make notes to prepare for partner chat.
> ❏ Write an entry in your reader's or writer's notebook.
> ❏ Work on your independent writing.
> ❏ Revise your "books I want to read" list.
> ❏ Work on your "ideas for writing" list.

Figure 3–1   *Independence chart in fifth-grade classroom*

In Lisbeth Arce's eighth-grade classes, students spent time discussing how they could get to their meeting area quickly and without infringing on others' rights to sit where they were comfortable. They discussed how they could be sure everyone was listening to the teacher's lesson and how they could help classmates who needed extra time. Lisbeth has impressed on them that time is important, so they have agreed to the following.

⬧ Students will come into the room and meet Lisbeth in the teaching area without delay (try to beat the bell).

⬧ If there are changes in what they need to bring or do, Lisbeth will write that on the white board in a designated space.

⬧ If someone forgets a book or notebooks, he or she agrees to do the work anyway (for example, do the reading work with another book, write on sheet of paper, borrow pen from peer).

⬧ Five students volunteer to coach others who might need to hear the lesson again—they will not coach a close friend to avoid chatting.

⬧ One student takes attendance and slips it to the teacher.

⬧ Homework is ongoing reading and writing; if it needs to be collected, there is a basket for that.

⬧ Each student signs up for an independent project of his or her choice (Figure 3–2)—they can work on it if time permits.

After looking at classroom of independent learners, Table 3–2 shows some ways we could answer teacher questions about independence.

Table 3–2 Frequently Asked Questions About How to Manage Student Independence

Teacher Questions	How Independence Helps
What about students who don't get started working and fool around?	Have students figure out their cues for getting started and revise them if they are not working.
How can I be sure they are really doing their work?	Trust them. Beyond that, they know you will meet with them in small groups and conferences and see their work.
How can I keep the class quiet enough to work?	When they are engaged in fascinating work that moves quickly, the noise—if any—will be work related.
How can I expect them to work on their own without a teacher watching them?	You can't watch them every minute, so you have to teach them to work on their own and to enjoy producing work for itself.
How can I turn my back?	They must trust and love you and you must do the same.
How can I keep track of what they are doing, especially if it differs from student to student?	Keep careful notes; check in with students frequently; keep conferring notes current; ask to see work regularly.
How can I know they'll "get it" in a short lesson?	Students with independence know they can stay back for more teaching or leave if they understand what to do. They also know that deep learning won't happen right away; they are comfortable with asking for help later on.

It is important that independence comes from the students—that is, it is not a series of assignments imposed by the teacher. So I would not suggest that teachers say, "After you finish your writing for today, do your vocabulary work, then read to a partner, and then practice spelling," and so on. This merely becomes a list of assignments, and in some cases, really just busywork or placeholders. Independent work must come from student interests: students decide what they would like to do in the five or ten

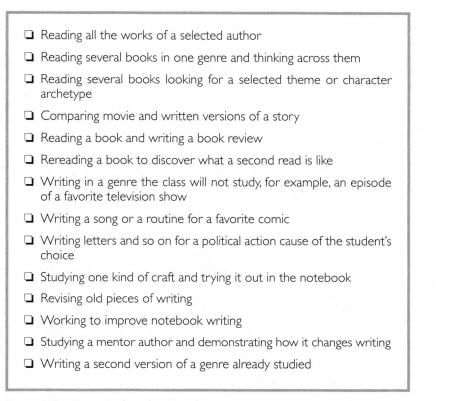

❏ Reading all the works of a selected author

❏ Reading several books in one genre and thinking across them

❏ Reading several books looking for a selected theme or character archetype

❏ Comparing movie and written versions of a story

❏ Reading a book and writing a book review

❏ Rereading a book to discover what a second read is like

❏ Writing in a genre the class will not study, for example, an episode of a favorite television show

❏ Writing a song or a routine for a favorite comic

❏ Writing letters and so on for a political action cause of the student's choice

❏ Studying one kind of craft and trying it out in the notebook

❏ Revising old pieces of writing

❏ Working to improve notebook writing

❏ Studying a mentor author and demonstrating how it changes writing

❏ Writing a second version of a genre already studied

Figure 3–2   *Types of independent projects*

or fifteen minutes they have left. This understanding is critical and brings home to them that all the reading and writing we teach them is not for the teacher—it is so they can use reading and writing to create a place in the world. It is so they can use the tools of reading and writing to become creative thinkers on their own. Of course, if a student decides that she wants to study spelling during her independent time and at some point will share with peers what she's done, that is legitimate independent work.

Clearly, independence is not taught in one lesson. It is a way to live in the room and of course a way to live outside of school. We model and coach independence. We listen to their suggestions for how to be independent and ways they would like to demonstrate their independence. We use independence as a positive factor in the room. We discuss it in class meetings and include it on assessments. Mostly, we assume that all students can do this, just as they can all learn to brush their teeth and feed themselves independently. As they need us less, they own their learning. And we have time for more teaching and conferring.

Rehearsal and Performance

Earlier we saw that teachers like Rachel, Paul, and Lisbeth have their students rehearse routines so they work smoothly and with ease. Rehearsal is important for performance of any kind. No musician would stand on stage to perform without hours of rehearsal, and we, the audience, would feel cheated if he did!

We owe our students the best performances as well, so I recommend that we rehearse our minilessons. Ten to fifteen minutes spent rehearsing lets us see where a lesson is weak, where transitions aren't working, and if the demonstration makes sense. We don't need to script every lesson, but there might be certain phrases we will use to clarify the concept. I always like to speak aloud a lesson in the quiet of my bedroom—the sound of my voice lets me hear potential problems. It's helpful to hear the words I plan to use and to revise them if necessary. Finally, I don't feel professional if the actual presentation of a lesson is the first time I've done it!

In many ways, teaching is performance. We consider our audience before we begin. We create conditions where the audience will be comfortable and anticipate our teaching work. We work off the audience's energy—it is hard to perform for a dull, lifeless, or apathetic audience. We shift our work depending on what the audience gives us. We enjoy watching the audience respond. We consider the many messages the audience gets from our words, our appearance, our body language, and our facial expressions. And sometimes, we deserve an Oscar.

Once when I was teaching fourth grade in New York City, I had a rare opportunity to take my class to a morning rehearsal of the New York Philharmonic at Avery Fisher Hall. I could hardly contain my excitement, and I prepared the class for weeks ahead. When we filed into our seats (left stage boxes!), the students were thrilled. In childish whispers they pointed out the architecture, the musicians, the instruments, the plush chairs, and so on. To my horror, the conductor looked up with annoyance a few times. Then he finally stopped the rehearsal and pointed up at me and my class. "All of you," he shouted. "Get out! Right now! Out!" We were ushered out in humiliation, some of us with tears in our eyes.

Of course, I realize this conductor was rehearsing his orchestra and was distracted by our quiet chatter. As teachers, we too are distracted by noise. Usually we have dignified ways to deal with it so we can get back to work. But this conductor didn't have coping mechanisms, and he neglected two important things. One was the feelings of the audience—our humiliation stung and made some students react in anger, others in shame, a few in childish posturing. The other was the negative effect his angry dismissal could have on the students' long-lasting attitude toward serious music—many of them will never go to a concert again, even if they have the choice.

From this experience, I learned that my response to my audience—my class—during a lesson tells them a great deal about what I believe about them. If I give my best performance, they may give their best learning. If I neglect the feelings of the class, some may react in humiliation, shame, or anger. Part of my work as a teacher is to be sure this doesn't happen, so I will not be derailed by student silliness. The other is that I never want youngsters to believe that they are not worthy of what I have to give. That may lead them to never want to feast on reading and writing again. Rehearsing lessons helps me perform with confidence so that I am not rattled by noise, interruption, broken equipment, and so on. The show goes on. The teaching continues.

You may consider rehearsing whole-class teaching the following ways.

- Imagine the class: Who are the students you want to check with during processing time? Where will they be sitting? Will students need to sit with partners or small groups? Who needs your gentle support?

- How will you orchestrate the physical layout of the presentation? Where will the chart paper need to be located? The overhead projector or Smart Board?

- How can you weave in language or information you have taught before?

- What are technical, encouraging, or other words you want to use? Do you need to write cues for yourself?

- When and how will you point out previous charts? Where are they located?

- When you write in front of the class, make sure you have already written the piece. Make it look as if you are writing extemporaneously, but be sure you can actually accomplish what you hope to teach in the lesson.

- Time the lesson. Is it close to ten to fifteen minutes? No doubt it will take longer in the actual performance.

- Anticipate problems or questions and have answers prepared or use them to revise your lesson.

Reteaching—Always We Begin Again

When I taught middle school, by a fluke of scheduling there was a small group of students who had me as their English teacher for sixth, seventh, and eighth grades. I remember being enraged when these students told me in eighth grade that they had never been taught a particular grammar point. After all, I had taught it to them in sixth and seventh grades! How could they say they never learned it? Of course, they were not lying at all. They were young students, and what seemed a pivotal concept to me was just one more lesson to them. This made me assess the effectiveness of my teaching and helped me learn an important lesson. In teaching, we begin again and again.

We teach *children*, even those of us who teach middle schoolers, who are just children in large bodies. They are novices at doing things we take for granted. We have been reading and writing much longer than they have, yet sometimes we forget. Sometimes we dissolve into frustration when students don't seem to learn things as quickly as we think we did. They forget to bring supplies, or their notebooks, or their pencils, or they tell us they don't "get it," or never learned it, or don't want to do it. And so we begin again.

Sometimes our teaching is not as effective as we had hoped—so we begin again. Sometimes a lesson does not go well—we being again. Sometimes we lose energy and become bogged down by all we are required to do—but we begin again. In Chapter 7 we will examine the process of reteaching. For now, I hope that acknowledging that we must reteach will bring a measure of comfort to our work.

Summary

We cannot be in all places at all times, though sometimes it feels as if we need to be omniscient. In order for classrooms to work, we must set routines in place without rigidity, understanding that the routines are to assist classroom workings, not to become the classroom workings. Furthermore, the goal is to "put ourselves out of a job" (figuratively, of course) so that students become independent learners who can carry on without input from us every two minutes. And because teaching is careful and deliberate, it makes sense for teachers to rehearse lessons to fine tune them. Elegance takes time and effort. Although we hope all minilessons will do their work, there will be times when we will have to reteach, sometimes to the whole class, more often in small groups or individually. There is an old adage that says "teaching is reteaching." We know it is more than that, but certainly that is one small piece of it.

For teachers to do

- Ask students to help you imagine routines that would keep the class running smoothly without being burdensome.

- Make a chart of routines; practice them with the class; revise them.

- Be sure to focus more on what each routine is meant to accomplish rather than the routine itself.

- Teach independence from the first day of school; help students own their learning.

- Know students well so that you can help them choose an independent project; most students will be able to do this on their own.

- With the class, make a chart of possible independent activities in addition to the project; always emphasize choice.

- Rehearse minilessons; work on the clarity of each part; be ready for the performance.

The Art of the Minilesson
or Time Well Spent

In her normal conversational voice, Rachel Moramarco says to her students, "I see that you are ready for writing. Let's come together to get started." Students gather, bringing supplies they know they might need. They sit around her on benches and on a rug. Rachel gathers them with dignity and grace—it is time for the excitement of learning something new. We all are part of it, and we will all be changed by the experience. Then she begins her carefully planned and rehearsed teaching.

A fine minilesson is a work of art. It is as careful and thoughtful as a symphony, with a structure and attention to detail, harmony, and theme. Rachel prepares her students for learning not by yelling at them or telling them it's time to get busy, but readying them for the joy of work.

As we turn our attention to the practice of teaching day by day and across the school year, we will examine daily challenges in classrooms and offer ways to deal with difficulty and discern occasions to celebrate. We must dig inside our own thinking and beliefs to reconsider the difference between clear teaching and muddy lessons that confuse students. Just as important is the need to *teach* something in the minilesson—it is not merely assigning work, or telling personal stories, or checking up on homework. Teaching is creating the conditions for learning and then presenting material that is carefully chosen to entice and deepen student knowledge without confusing or overwhelming. Lessons must have depth and breadth, that is, they must be clear and understandable at the moment but also contain opportunities for deeper and longer thought over time. A good lesson takes fifteen minutes but lasts a long time.

In this chapter, we will examine minilessons, which are the jewel of whole-class teaching. We'll look at the following points.

◈ how minilessons help manage time

◈ teaching one thing at a time

◈ the basic structure of a minilesson

How Minilessons Help Manage Time

I confess with dismay that in my early years as a teacher, I was the queen of the forty-minute lesson. I could go on with multiple examples of what I thought I was teaching, in addition to multiple teaching points, until I finally stopped babbling just as the bell rang. It was my own one-person show. I'm sure my students nearly fell off their chairs from boredom, unless they were surreptitiously doing their French homework. And then I learned from Lucy Calkins that *time is all we have*, and my attitude changed from filling up time with my talk to using every minute wisely. Enter the minilesson and workshop teaching.

Now I recognize that the purpose of a session is to teach something small but significant that all students can then actually practice doing. So simple, but so profound. Within this structure, there is time allocated for whole-group instruction, small-group instruction (guided reading or writing, strategy lessons), and individual instruction (conferring). When each of these types of instruction are in place, we have the best chance for meeting all students' needs and for getting to know each learner and his needs well. This means that whole-class instruction must be short, targeted, and broad enough for all students' needs.

A minilesson is the opportunity to gather students together for a short time and have their complete attention. In these days of sound bytes and video games, and a world that moves so quickly with sound and color, we are challenged to keep some students engaged. In addition, teachers often tell me that they do not have enough time for all they have to do. One benefit a minilesson offers is forcing us to make careful use of time, forcing us to compress teaching. It requires us to avoid long digressions and engagement with disruptions, which always increase the risk of losing students' interest. This teaching is sharp, clear, and focused. And although the lessons are short, they provide opportunity for differentiation for all students—challenging some and launching others into deeper work.

How short is short? The general time frame for a minilesson is ten to fifteen minutes. Of course, there will be times when it may go longer, but these must be the exception rather than the rule. The more time we spend with students around us, the less time they actually spend reading or writing. The more time we spend going over and over a concept, the more we risk losing the students who got it in the first place. And students who need extra support will receive it at the end of the lesson anyway. There is little reason to prolong a lesson.

I always advise teachers to audiotape their minilessons. Then listen to them. Can you identify each component of the lesson? Can you assess whether each component did its part? What type of language do you use? Where do you get distracted? What conditions do you need to establish before beginning? And where do you misuse time or use it well? How can you work to sound more natural? Which are the weak and strong parts of your lessons?

Let's imagine a typical forty-five-minute block of time for reading. The teacher gathers students to teach a minilesson on a reading strategy, mostly likely from her observations of what students need, plus considering standards and the district curriculum. The minilesson, following the format just described, takes fifteen minutes. This means that she has the remaining half hour to meet with small groups and individuals. It also means that students have a half hour to actually *read*. Some students will meet with the teacher for small-group or individual instruction, but many students will have the time to read (or write during writing workshop). Imagine the benefits in learning to read if we provided time for students to read; imagine learning to write by writing. By the way, this is not "sustained silent reading" or "DEAR" (drop everything and read) time. It is *directed reading or writing*, during which students practice reading/writing strategies that have been taught in the lesson, and the teacher continues with other types of instruction. This makes maximum use of the allotted time, because the class is working while the teacher continues with differentiated instruction.

Here is one possible time frame for a forty-five-minute workshop.

◈ minilesson with entire class—fifteen minutes

◈ small-group instruction while others read or write—ten minutes

◈ individual instruction (conferring) while others read or write—fifteen minutes

❖ share time and transitions (whole class)—five minutes

In a school with a block schedule for reading and writing, teachers may have 90 to 120 minutes for reading and writing. Again, the minilesson remains at fifteen minutes each for reading and for writing. The other time is spent with additional small-group instruction and conferring, and possibly tending to other district mandates, such as word work and spelling instruction. The minilesson ensures that there is instruction in reading and writing every day, but that the instruction does not preempt actual reading and actual writing.

Looking back at the structure for minilessons is helpful for keeping track of time. For example, the greeting will take less than a minute, as may the orientation or link. Obviously the teaching component will take longest, but not so long that there is little time for processing and reteaching. Considering time elements forces us to make teaching lean and clean. I listen to tapes of my teaching from years ago and I cringe at how much time I wasted—digressions, responding to announcements, correcting students, adding personal stories, and so on. Wasted minutes for which I ask forgiveness from former students. Now I measure my words— I rehearse my lessons. I've even scripted them for practice, though I believe teaching from the script is unnatural and kills spontaneity.

Teaching One Thing at a Time

There is so much to teach. Teachers say this all the time and they are right. How do we know what to teach across 180 days of school? There are units of study, curriculum maps, and standards to guide us, but many of our decisions come from studying student work What do students already know and what do they need to know? Which information or skills fit best into small-group or individual instruction, and which are significant enough that the whole class needs instruction? Teachers face these choices every day. Minilessons may be short, but they must be good enough to carry the major part of the class's learning.

Here are guidelines for determining the content of a minilesson.

❖ includes only one teaching point

❖ small but significant content

❖ flexible enough so that all levels of students can accomplish it

- part of a series of lessons that extend from it, or it extends from a previous lesson

- usually belongs to a unit of study

- teaches students to be better readers and writers

- appropriate to the grade level and unit of study

The penultimate point on this list comes from the work of Lucy Calkins and Donald Murray, as well as other great educators, who for so long have told us to "teach the writer, not the writing; teach the reader, not the reading." This means that our lessons must make students better readers and writers in general, not just provide minor information that will help them for one day or for one piece of writing (or reading). It sets the bar quite high for us, meaning lessons must have a lasting effect on students. Our teaching must become wise and profound.

Notice that the minilesson in Figure 4–1 is about something *small* enough that all students can handle it, yet *significant* enough that it can have major implications for students' writing. Some students may follow through in the barest way, and yet they will have practiced an important

---

❏ needs of students gleaned from careful observation, conferring, and other assessments

❏ how the teaching point fits into the unit of study, district mandates, standards, and so on

❏ literature or your own writing to be used for modeling

❏ how to isolate a concept in order to teach it; exactly name your teaching point in one sentence

❏ whether the teaching point is small enough to do in one day but significant enough to continue to be explored and deepened over time

❏ what you expect students to be able to do at the end of the workshop

❏ how you will look for continued evidence that your teaching is effective

❏ possibilities for differentiation

❏ whether students are ready for the lesson or need additional teaching first

Figure 4-1 *What to consider when planning a minilesson*

strategy for all writing and thinking work. Some may be so intrigued by the idea that they will play with multiple categories, or try the strategy in science and social studies, or arrive at breakthrough thinking about their topics. The lesson is appropriate for all students, yet flexible enough for students to apply it in their own way to their own topics. One important criterion for good lessons is that they appear simple, but they are never simplistic. Good teaching looks easy but has multilayered effects on students and ripples over time to affect learning in many ways, including across content areas. The structure helps us to make teaching accessible to the whole class.

On the other hand, it is so easy to pile on too much information when we teach. We teach one good thing, but then we remind students about their spelling and their handwriting, and their homework and their vocabulary, and no sharpening pencils or going to the bathroom . . . and before we know it, they are asking us what we want them to do. This is a legitimate question from children. It's as if they are saying, "Of all the items you just sprinkled on us in the last few minutes, which do you really want us to do? And what was the lesson about? Because we forgot!"

So teach one point and only one point. Save other good lessons for another day. Plan a series of lessons that flow from one another. For example, the lesson on categories might be followed by lessons on types of categories, how to decide if the categories are robust or not, adding or deleting information from categories, and writing up each category as a chunk or paragraph, under a subtitle, or as a page of a picture book. Don't give in to the panicked feeling that you have to teach them everything!

In addition, minilessons can draw their content from many different learning needs. We often think that lessons must only deal with facts or information, but this isn't so. For example, I could teach several angles on revision in a minilesson:

- specific strategies for revising writing (writing)

- when and how to revise (process)

- using a mentor author (literature in writing)

- discerning revision needs and trying out possibilities (thinking)

- conferring with revision partner (workshop procedure)

From this we see that minilessons are more than relaying facts and information. They can include lessons on the writing process, getting ideas for writing, how to use literature when writing, thinking skills (habits of mind), routines and procedures, community building, and so on. The litmus test is whether the teaching point will carry enough weigh to make it significant all year long.

Teachers who keep charts of their minilessons create an archive of information for students and others to access when needed. One way that students can "read the room" is to refer to charts of previous minilessons and apply them to their current learning. This helps students become independent learners, and it teaches them that every lesson is important, so important that we create a record and refer back to it. Teachers should refer back to previous lessons when orienting students to a new lesson. During conferences or small-group instruction, pointing to charts of previous lessons helps build scaffolds for students. We hope that all lessons are connected in some way—whether by topic, or thinking skill, or usefulness across genre or content areas, but we must deliberately make these connections for students so that they begin to see that all learning is woven together. Teachers should regularly say things like, "Remember when we studied careful word choice in poetry? Well, let's think about that as we write our feature articles." When they help students make these cognitive leaps, they teach students that every lesson matters and every lesson can show up again at some point in the year. Learning is cumulative and complex. It's a sad thing to have to miss a day of school.

The Basic Structure of the Minilesson

I like to think of the structure of a minilesson in terms of sonata form in music. The composers of the classical and early romantic eras wrote gorgeous symphonies, string quartets, overtures, concerti, and so on, using a form, or structure, that was clear though flexible. Some of the clarity and beauty of Mozart and Haydn's works are found in their adherence to this form while allowing their creativity to soar under its careful constraints. Like sonata form, the form of a minilesson provides structure within which teachers do their finest and smartest teaching. Like great composers, teachers compose their art—their teaching—within the structure of the minilesson.

Teachers know that careful lesson planning is one key to fine teaching. (Other keys include assessment, use of standards and curriculum mapping, and so on.) Often planning a lesson includes deciding on the content of the lesson, creating an activity for students, and some kind of follow-up. But good teaching is more than content, activity, and follow-up—there are so many factors to consider. What is the essential teaching point in this lesson? What about time? What do students already know? How will the content of this lesson build on prior lessons and prepare for future lessons? How can we make difficult concepts clear? How will we assess student learning? The basic structure of a minilesson helps us with some of these factors (Figure 4–2). The idea of dividing a minilesson into structural components was born at the Teachers College Reading and Writing

It is important to note that other educators have also deconstructed minilessons and assigned names to the various parts. Although the names of the components may differ slightly, their ideas are sound and smart (Calkins 2000). It matters less which author's structure you choose to follow; it is more important to internalize that minilessons are purposeful, highly defined teaching tools, not merely short instructions to a class!

Greeting or invitation: The greeting is an invitation to learn, a polite way to begin any conversation. The teacher initiates a formal learning meeting, establishes the intent of the session, and shows his excitement about the upcoming lesson. The greeting is short.

Orientation or link: The teacher reorients students to learning by reminding them of previous lessons, referring to recent charts and discussions, and/or citing books they've read or studied. Having established a context for the day's lesson, the teacher states the exact purpose for the lesson. Often he will have the purpose written for students to see and refer to later.

Teaching: The teacher teaches a concept, strategy, process, or fact either by modeling or demonstrating. This may include using his own writing or reading, or referring to a mentor text. On rare occasions, the teacher may model by using a student's writing, but only with the student's permission. The teaching often involves thinking aloud and writing in front of the students.

Processing or evaluation: The teacher gives students the opportunity to "try on" what he has just taught. This may include partner conversations, a quick try-it in their notebooks, searching through their drafts or folders, or other work. The purpose is to prepare students for their upcoming class work and for the teacher to survey the class to determine the degree of understanding. Often the teacher will listen to several partner groups talking or taking notes or will glance at student writing over shoulders. The teacher takes notes and then decides what type of clarification or reteaching is needed.

Reteaching or clarification: Based on his observations during the processing time, the teacher tells students his impression of what they need. He talks about his sense of what the class has grasped, and he may reteach the concept. Often he will share what students said or did or may ask students to share. This may include ways students pushed their understanding or tried to anticipate difficulty.

Charge to the class: Based on the minilesson, the teacher tells the class the specific work for the day. Although most students will do the assigned work, the teacher provides opportunities for choice. Some students will immediately use the day's minilesson during their work time; others may not use it that day, but the next or in a week or month. Some students will think about when they will use the lesson; they may practice is immediately to remember it, or they may plan to use it on another day. Frequently the charge to the class will contain a preview of the next lesson or ways to deepen or challenge students.

Closing: The teacher asks a student to repeat the work for the day, refers to the written purpose, and invites students who have questions to stay for an "instant replay" of the lesson. The closing is short.

Figure 4–2 *Basic structure of a minilesson*

Some teachers are wary of writing in front of their students during a minilesson or of demonstrating reading strategies from their own reading. It is not easy to put ourselves on the line this way. But our demonstrations become authentic and honest when we share our struggles with students. No, the teacher is not perfect, nor does he have all the answers. Furthermore, demonstration writing does not need to be prize-worthy; in fact, it would intimidate most students if it were. However, if teachers fear writing because they feel uncomfortable with certain genres, or with grammatical structures, and so on, then this indicates areas where they will want to focus effort for their own learning. We can't teach feature articles, for example, if we don't know what they are and haven't tried to write one ourselves. So I encourage you to relax and trust yourself and your students, and then to challenge yourself to learn more about writing.

Project. Lucy Calkins' work on this is seminal; she uses the term *architecture* of a minilesson to designate each part of a minilesson (Calkins et al. 2003).

Each of the components of a minilesson has a function. The greeting brings students together and invites them to learn. The charge tells them exactly what to do that day. The teaching part is clear, and it includes some demonstration of what they should do. Teaching is not merely telling, as Lucy Calkins has taught us.

Look at Figure 4–3 for a transcript of a minilesson to examine the components.

In naming discrete parts of a minilesson, I fear teachers may become burdened by them. I hope this is not the case. As with any new learning, such as playing an instrument, beginning a sport, or learning to drive, the steps of the process seem hard and carry

---

Greeting: Good morning writers. Thank you for inviting me to your classroom today for writing workshop. [*Teacher establishes a pleasant and friendly tone.*]

Orientation or link: Yesterday on the phone, your teacher told me that you are preparing to write nonfiction picture books for third through sixth graders. That sounds great and I'd love to see them when they are done. She told me that you are taking lots of notes as you prepare to write, and I notice that you have a list posted here of the topics each of you has chosen. I also see a chart on types of resources and ways to take notes, like index cards and keeping a notebook. She also told me that your notes seem to be getting out of control, so I think it's a good idea to talk about note taking today. Specifically, let's look at how writers use categories in their note taking, which helps organize their writing later on. [*Teacher establishes why she has chosen to teach this lesson.*]

Teaching: I am working on something in my notebook. It started as a bunch of entries, but now I know it's going to grow into something bigger. I've been thinking a lot about chocolate and it could become an essay. Even though I'm not sure of the genre yet—and it could become a picture book—I've been taking notes. I've been writing a lot in my notebook and doing some field research (you know, eating lots of chocolate), but while that was fun, it wasn't helping me to get deeper into my topic. So I decided that making some categories that might help me get to the heart of my thinking. Now because writers use their notes before they start composing a draft, my notes really need to help me figure out what I'm going to say. So the categories are really important for me to know how to organize this writing. [*puts up chart with categories on it and reads them*] So here are some categories I am considering for my topic:

❏ My mother and chocolate.

❏ What I like about dark chocolate and how I search for the best.

Figure 4–3   *The components of a minilesson: grade 5 writing workshop minilesson transcript on using categories to help note taking*

❑ Looking for the connection with my mother … Genes? Nurture? Comfort?

❑ Should there be a whole section on my chocolate obsession?

❑ Does it signify the rise from poverty? Chocolate was scarce when we were poor, but now I can be eating Godiva chocolate and going to France.... Does chocolate mean that I'm not poor anymore?

❑ History of chocolate.

❑ Health benefits.

❑ Folklore.

Student: What about rumors?

Teacher: Yes, yes! Rumors about chocolate! Like: "If you eat chocolate you have greater chance of winning next election." *[adds rumors to the chart]*

❑ Description = sweet? All I have is that it's sweet, so I have some work to do there.

I think I have too many categories here, so I probably will have to combine some of them. But for now, the categories are a good way to get me thinking about chocolate in expansive ways and to help me see what information I need to gather. I can see where I need to find more information—like the description of chocolate—and I can see where I am going off on silly tangents—like no one really cares about my chocolate obsession. *[Teacher uses her own writing to demonstrate point of lesson that note taking helps organize thinking.]*

Processing or quick evaluation: So right now would you please think about your topic. *[waits about a half minute]* Try to think of at least two categories or parts of it that could help you gather information. Let's take time to think about that for one minute. *[waits]* Now please share your categories or your thinking with a partner. *[Teacher listens to three groups. Teacher gives students opportunity to process and she listens for problems or extensions to learning.]*

Reteaching: OK, let's come back together. While I was listening in to your conversation, I heard a few interesting things. Marley and Anne said that you have to be careful about the categories you choose because if you don't choose wisely, you can go off on a tangent. That's very true. We'll need to be careful about that. And Suze and Rick said that just talking with a partner helped them to name a few categories they might use. So talking might be a good strategy for you. *[Teacher validates students' concerns and uses them to warn others.]*

Charge to the class: What I would like you to try today is to make a list of possible categories that might help you with your topic. Try to name three categories and then consider whether they are good, strong categories that might help you find lots of information. Some categories you will decide are not important enough and you will cross them off your list. But I hope you will find at least three categories that will work for you. You can write these in your notebook or on index cards. Once you are sure of them, you can start using them to help you research. *[Teacher tells the class the work for the day. She also foreshadows the next lesson, which will be on how to evaluate the quality of the categories.]*

Closing: Are there any questions? Do you all know what to do? Good. Someone please repeat our work for today. *[One student repeats charge to class, as teacher writes it on sentence strip.]* OK, you can go to your places and begin. If you need to hear this again, you can ask Sharon or Geoffrey, or stay with me for an instant replay. *[Teacher provides multiple opportunities to see and hear the task for the day and provides opportunity for help with it.]*

Figure 4–3   (Continued)

most of our attention at first. How do you hold a violin bow? How do you get the basketball into the hoop? How do you make a left turn? And how on earth do you parallel park? Of course, these matters become second nature to us as we practice and move on to other skills. We hardly think about them anymore. It is the same with minilessons. The structure becomes routine and we focus on other ways to hone our whole-class teaching. So I encourage you to plan with these components in mind, and listen to audiotapes of your lessons to identify where you transitioned from one part to another, and study to make each part more successful. Be assured that eventually the components will become natural to you and be merely tools to help you teach.

Summary

The minilesson is an exquisite tool for teaching that is clear and concise. The structure and time constraints of minilessons force us to be thoughtful, planful, and deliberate about teaching. There can be no wasted words or wasted time. The short duration of the lessons provides time for other types of instruction—yet minilessons are not easy. They are elegant, like string quartets, and profound in their clarity and depth. Although not an easy way to teach, the long-term benefits of minilessons make them worth studying and practicing.

For teachers to do

- Plan a minilesson; then audiotape and study it. Ask a colleague to listen to it and give you feedback. The form or outline of a minilesson should help frame how the content will be delivered. For example, in order to decide what the "link" is, teachers need to have a sense of the order of teaching, of student needs (content and differentiation), and of how to connect one lesson to the next, to the larger unit, and to learning goals in general.

- Plan for content, but then consider how the content fits into the larger unit and learning goals, for example, in poetry, we want students to understand how important word choice is, and so on.

- Practice the form of a minilesson, while noticing how it makes your teaching clearer.

- Make a list of possible minilessons and then reread the list to decide on a logical order, lessons that are supportive, optional lessons, and key lessons that may need to be retaught in various ways (small groups, different angle on subsequent day).

- Some lessons are "main idea" lessons and others are "supporting" lessons. Know and plan in advance for each and be sure to include both kinds. For example, a main lesson on paying attention to the sounds of words may be followed by three supportive lessons on onomatopoeia, assonance, and alliteration. The main lesson is critical to establishing context for the others, and it may include inquiry and discussion.

- In every outline for a unit of study, there must be room for revision. Based on assessment of student work, teachers may have to reteach or focus on a lesson before continuing. Be careful not to get sidetracked so that the unit stretches out far longer than you'd planned. It is better to teach less and teach it well than to "get it all in," which could frustrate or bore students.

- Remember that all good teaching is, in some way, teaching "for the test." In essence, understand how each lesson will help students become better writers and readers in the long run.

5

Studying Whole-Class Instruction to Deepen and Refine It

Each time I visit Sarah Daunis' classroom, I learn something new about challenging, ethical, and compassionate teaching. Today she is teaching her fifth graders about punctuation, specifically, how to punctuate dialogue. They are writing personal narratives, and Sarah knows that including dialogue will help add meaning to their stories. In the first of a series of minilessons on punctuation, she shows them a page from a read-aloud book they've shared, *The Golden Compass* (2006) by Philip Pullman, and they discuss how the punctuation marks help them to understand which character is talking. Sarah pushes them to realize that punctuating dialogue is not arbitrary; knowing the meaning of the punctuation marks' positions makes a difference in navigating a written conversation. Students nod as she speaks, showing they understand what she is saying. They process this information with their partners as Sarah listens, and then they go off to practice writing dialogue for their stories using conventional punctuation. Several students choose to rehearse by reading through dialogue chunks in their books before trying to write; others keep a text close by for reference. Sarah's teaching has the global thinking that makes teaching great: teaching that works for the day, looks toward the future, and allows for student differences.

Sarah's work is beautiful. She has decided on the content based on student need. She has woven read-aloud, independent reading, and writing needs together. She has taken into account lessons that will come after this one. She teaches something critically important in reading and writing and shows students a way to become independent with it. She gives support to students who may need extra time, and challenges a few who are ready for extra information. Her teaching is ethical because it is filled with respect for students as learners, as humans, and as thinkers. Her manner as well as her global vision and thoughtful planning are what help her to teach successfully. One of the great joys of my work is learning from a wise and generous teacher like her.

Keeping Sarah's teaching and what we can learn from her in mind, this chapter will focus on ways to deepen, broaden, and get the most from minilessons. We'll explore the following:

- minilesson themes, variations, and development

- content choices that scaffold and extend learning

- making time in a minilesson to give gracious support to all learners

Minilesson Themes, Variations, and Development

In my early days as a reading and writing workshop teacher, I "went with the flow." In some ways, I was much attuned to the needs of my students (good), but I confess that with every new staff development workshop I attended, I switched gears in my teaching (bad). Although I was always on my toes, I know that my teaching lacked depth. My lessons were what are now called "popcorn" lessons, meaning I popped up with something new every day. It was impulsive, carpe diem teaching. I loved it. But I was a novice and had so much to learn.

Reading and writing workshop teaching was in its infancy then, and fortunately, we have learned a great deal about rigorous and wise teaching. We are smarter about molding student needs together with standards and curricular mandates. We have adopted units of study. We have fallen in love with conventions again. We know more about teaching thinking and about studying our own teaching to get better. We're like the musician or athlete who works to refine one piece of her performance, whether it is her footwork, her bow stroke, her speed, her phrasing. For teachers, this translates into taking apart our teaching bit by bit and studying which parts of it need our attention. We are always learning, always refining. This is the challenge and the fun. In this section, we will explore one way to refine teaching by planning lessons that make teaching last and challenge students' thinking skills.

Theme and Development

Earlier in this book, I mentioned "sonata form" as one way composers organized first movements of symphonies, concerti, string quartets, and so on, during the classical music era. One of the fascinating aspects of sonata form is that it introduces a theme, or musical idea, and then develops it. We can borrow this structure as one way to organize groups of related, rather than single, minilessons. Like a symphony, a group of related minilessons might start with the exposition of a theme, or general concept, followed by exploration and development of it. When planning for whole-class instruction that is grounded and deep, this might translate into a group of related minilessons like those in Figure 5-1. The chart in Figure 5-1 shows a hierarchical relationship between these lessons. Minilesson #1 introduces the concept of adding dialogue to personal narrative, while the subordinate minilessons develop other points about the use of dialogue. What remains important is that the theme is not alone. It is supported by other lessons that add depth and breadth to it. We avoid teaching stand-alone lessons, because this often results in surface teaching. When we get on a line of thinking about a concept or a theme, it makes sense to stay with it for a few days. Some teachers call this an "arc" or "thread" of minilessons, as a way to indicate that an important concept is driving the teaching.

Knowing that we'll stay with an idea, or theme, for more than one day helps us to think about how to deepen it. It also supports students to

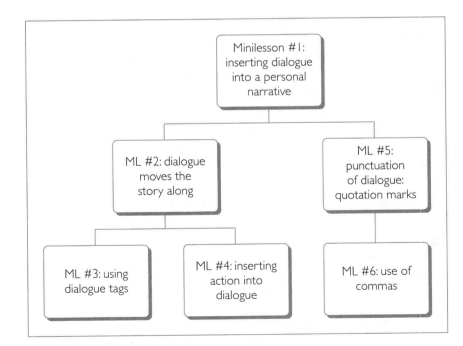

Figure 5-1   *Related minilessons*

learn concepts in depth, rather than jumping from one to the next to the next. For example, a lesson about "using ending punctuation when you write" deepens to "pay attention to the sound of your voice and use punctuation to cue your readers." This may be followed by lessons on rehearsing reading with punctuation, using a comma to write an introductory phrase, or making time to reflect on what you have noticed about punctuation. Thinking about related lessons would deepen all work. For example, revision minilessons might change from "revise your writing to add voice" to "*ways* to revise your language that will improve the voice in your writing." If you are working on voice, you will stay with it rather than moving from one lesson on voice to a lesson on something else, then something else again. Figure 5–2 shows several possibilities for theme and development lessons.

Designing theme and development minilessons allows a teacher to plan for deep study of a concept. Additional considerations for planning these groups of lessons help set guidelines or criteria for groups of minilessons, such as the following.

- The reading or writing minilesson theme is a major skill or strategy students need in workshop.

- Often the theme or concept is important in content area work also.

- The main theme or concept is useful in all or most units of study in reading and writing.

- It is a concept that will improve reading or writing across time and indefinitely.

Theme and Development	**Theme and Variations**
Minilessons that deepen and explore a teaching point in order to deepen knowledge, skill, or independence	Minilessons that provide variation on a teaching point in order to accumulate knowledge
Purpose is to provide depth of knowledge	Purpose is to build breadth of knowledge
Encourages students to revisit writing and go deeper into it	Layers on information, such as building a menu of strategies from which to choose

Figure 5–2   *Comparison of minilesson organizing structures*

Theme and Variations

Although sonata form was most important to classical era music, it was not the only organizational structure that composers used. Another structure was "theme and variations," which was often used for the second movement of a larger piece of music. True to its name, this structure presented a musical theme and then was followed by multiple variations on the theme, some of them quite creative. In terms of minilessons, this structure provides teachers with another tool for planning lessons: teach a major theme, and then follow it with variations. Theme and variations differs from theme and development form in one major way—theme and variation lessons are cumulative. Rather than going deeper and becoming more sophisticated, as in theme and development, the teacher adds more information in layers, building a menu of possibilities from which students can choose. It is important that we include both kinds of minilessons so that we build breadth and depth.

Both types of minilessons are important. If we study the possible minilesson chart (Figure 5–3), we see that in some cases, a lesson calls for us to layer on or accumulate information. For example, when initially teaching revision, we would want students to have multiple, quick strategies for revising. However, in some cases, we need minilessons that encourage students to go further and to understand a deeper purpose. So later on in revision study, we'd teach revision that is deliberate—less choosing from a menu of possibilities and more deciding what is needed, and why, and knowing how to figure out solutions independently. Figure 5–4 shows several theme and development lessons and Figure 5–5 shows several theme and variations lessons.

Knowing the structures for grouping minilessons is useful for organizing content for instruction. It is also helpful for going back to assess instruction. How can we be sure students have received enough depth of instruction if we cannot ensure that our teaching has depth and longevity? Although not every single minilesson must fit into a group or theme, keeping this organization as a general structure will improve instruction dramatically.

Content Choices That Scaffold and Extend Learning

Most teachers understand and agree that every teacher is a reading and writing teacher. Surely the technology teacher, the art teacher, the music

Theme and Development	Theme and Variations
How to use punctuation to elaborate and clarify	Inquiry study of punctuation: learning the marks and what they mean
How to use a notebook over time as a workbench for developing ideas, revising, and living like a writer	How to generate ideas for writing
Choosing words deliberately for clarity and sound	Ways to find and choose "juicy" words for writing
How to write in one genre, then the next	Ways to organize writing in any genre
Bringing qualities of good writing from one genre to the next	How to use punctuation, grammar, voice, and so on in a particular genre
Building independence in reading and writing	Ways to extend, or create meaning in, writing
How to work with a partner and/or a small group, such as a book club	Ways to begin (or end) writing
Going into deeper and more extensive revisions	How to write with voice

Figure 5–3   *Possible minilessons for theme and development versus theme and variations*

teacher, and so on have important roles to play in students learning the many literacies that are required in our global society. Teachers in self-contained classrooms often have a clear vision of how literacies intersect. For example, if students have difficulty reading the science textbook, perhaps they need to learn the literacy of textbook reading and how to extract information from a nonfiction text. Thus, classroom teachers know that they must teach students to read and write math, science, social studies, computer, as well as reading books and writing narratives.

As teachers, it is important to choose content for reading and writing minilessons based on how much we can get from each lesson. This refers back to deliberate teaching that is grounded in solid understanding of how we learn and what students need to know. It also pretty much eliminates the popcorn lessons. Minilessons must be thorough, clear, and concise. The strongest lessons will have an impact in many or all of the following areas.

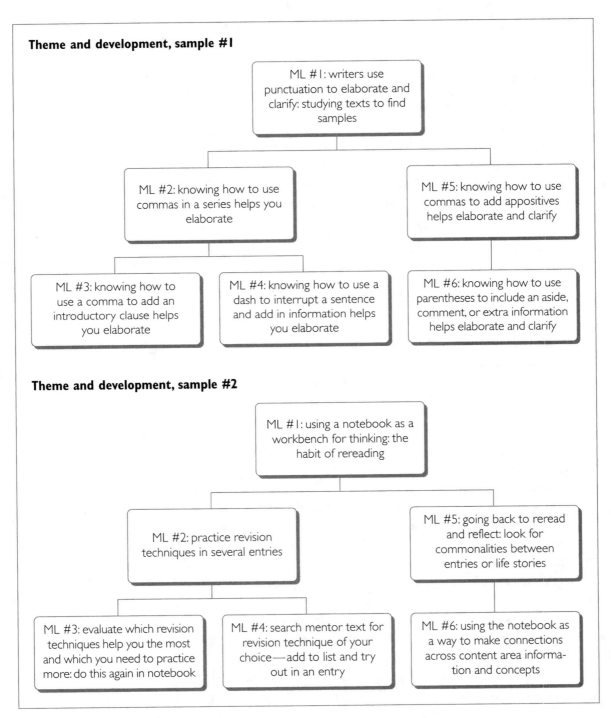

Theme and development, sample #1

ML #1: writers use punctuation to elaborate and clarify: studying texts to find samples

ML #2: knowing how to use commas in a series helps you elaborate

ML #5: knowing how to use commas to add appositives helps elaborate and clarify

ML #3: knowing how to use a comma to add an introductory clause helps you elaborate

ML #4: knowing how to use a dash to interrupt a sentence and add in information helps you elaborate

ML #6: knowing how to use parentheses to include an aside, comment, or extra information helps elaborate and clarify

Theme and development, sample #2

ML #1: using a notebook as a workbench for thinking: the habit of rereading

ML #2: practice revision techniques in several entries

ML #5: going back to reread and reflect: look for commonalities between entries or life stories

ML #3: evaluate which revision techniques help you the most and which you need to practice more: do this again in notebook

ML #4: search mentor text for revision technique of your choice—add to list and try out in an entry

ML #6: using the notebook as a way to make connections across content area information and concepts

Figure 5–4   *Theme and development minilessons*

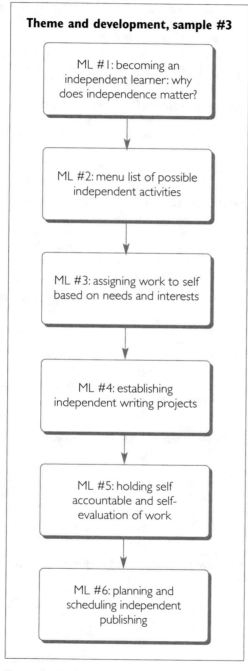

Theme and development, sample #3

ML #1: becoming an independent learner: why does independence matter?

↓

ML #2: menu list of possible independent activities

↓

ML #3: assigning work to self based on needs and interests

↓

ML #4: establishing independent writing projects

↓

ML #5: holding self accountable and self-evaluation of work

↓

ML #6: planning and scheduling independent publishing

Figure 5-4   (*Continued*)

Theme and variations, sample #1:
How to begin a piece of writing

Theme ML #1	Begin with a meaningful, thoughtful question.
ML #2	Begin with a surprise (onomatopoeia or strong statement).
ML #3	Begin in the middle of the action.
ML #4	Begin with a character saying something important.
ML #5	Begin with an opinion statement.
ML #6	Begin with a description of setting

Theme and variations, sample #2: How to end a piece of writing

Theme ML #1	End with a rhetorical question.
ML #2	End with a character saying something important.
ML #3	End with an opinion statement.
ML #4	End with a conclusion that actually "draws or concludes" from all the evidence presented.

Theme and variations, sample #3: How to organize writing

Theme ML #1	ABA form.
ML #2	Every day/one day.
ML #3	Write with an organizing repeating line.
ML #4	Write in groups of three, e.g., three paragraphs.
ML #5	Circular pattern

Theme and variations, sample #4: How to keep a notebook

Theme ML#1	Live like a writer; decorate the notebook to make it yours.
ML #2	Routines for writing in the notebook (certain time every day, when you finish work, for homework four times a week, and so on).
ML #3	Begin list of types of notebook entries: memories.
ML #4	Continue list: observations.
ML #5	Continue list: writing off others' writing.

Theme and variations, sample #5: Punctuation marks

Theme ML #1	Review ending punctuation.
ML #2	Use quotation marks in dialogue.
ML #3	Use quotation marks for a colloquial saying.
ML #4	Write a compound sentence using comma and conjunction.
ML #5	Write a compound sentence using semicolon and no conjunction.

Theme and variations, sample #6: Quick revision techniques

Theme ML #1	Pay attention to the sounds of words: add alliteration.
ML #2	Add examples in groups of three.
ML #3	Include a character's thoughts as well as actions.
ML #4	Add movement to dialogue.
ML #5	Play with sentence length to vary it.

Figure 5-5   *Theme and variations minilessons*

- transfer from one content area to another

- real-life application

- habits of mind

- qualities of good reading and writing

Transfer from One Content Area to Another

We must remember always that our work is to teach students to think. We use the medium of reading and writing to do this, but in reality, thinking is required all day, every day. The wisest and most long-lasting teaching is done when teachers make deliberate moves that show transfer from thinking in one content area, say, writing, to another area, say, science. One way to do this is through intertextuality, or teaching students to see similar features, ideas, characters, or metaphors in a variety of texts and a variety of content areas.

A sixth-grade class is studying the lives of famous women in social studies. Earlier in the year they had studied character traits in a short story unit of study in reading and writing. The teacher nudges them to use those character traits as a way to understand famous women. Students notice that Clara Barton was tenacious, Mother Teresa was single-minded, Lucretia Mott was courageous. All of them refused to follow accepted norms of "politeness." Students have used their knowledge of uncovering character traits to understand real-life characters.

A fifth-grade class is working on environmental issues in science. They are reading online articles and books on environmental issues and watching television shows at home that are dedicated to environmental awareness. Although the information is fascinating, some students have trouble reading the articles and books. The teacher does try to match them with comprehensible texts, but she also returns to the nonfiction reading and writing unit done in the fall. She reviews strategies for reading and writing nonfiction, such as features of nonfiction text, which she knows will be helpful for students in the current science unit.

This implication of the preceding examples is that smart teachers make sure their teaching is woven into a tapestry of instructional art. They see beyond the lesson of today or even the unit of the month to consider the interconnectedness of all instruction. This perspective certainly changes the lessons they decide to teach. They hold themselves and their students to spiral teaching and learning, where each lesson is important enough to be revisited at another time or in another content area. Figure 5–6 shows ways minilessons in reading and writing might be useful in other content areas. If we want to make the most of our teaching, we will focus on considering this as we plan instruction.

Teaching in every area is related. In the short time we have with students, we can ensure the most learning when we thoughtfully weave together learning in all content areas and when we remember that we teach all kinds of literacies to all types of students all day long.

Real-Life Application

In their classic book *Coping with Chaos* (1991), Brian Cambourne and Jan Turbill list several conditions for learning. One of these is that students must see real-life application in order to become invested in information. I see this in my own life. For example, I have no interest in playing golf; therefore, television shows on improving one's golf swing do not interest me in the least. I can hardly stay awake, whereas a close friend who lives for her golf game is on her feet and glued to every word of the TV instructor. There is no real-life application for me, but for her, it is exciting and fascinating. Of course, we cannot plan lessons that will span every student's personal interests, but knowing your students well and building those interests into your lessons as metaphors or modeling can be quite effective.

Putting personal interests aside, Turbill and Cambourne's theory does help us to frame instruction in a "you need to know this" way. We must not only teach students reading and writing, but we must show them how each lesson fits into the larger sense of what will make them succeed in other endeavors. For some students, knowing that reading and writing well will improve their video game scores (and vice versa, Gee 2004) may be the real-life application that makes the difference. For some, it may be sports, music, or art. For others, it may be the academic thrill of reading and writing—some students do become excited about becoming poets, songwriters, moviemakers, reporters, sportscasters, and so on. Whatever the interest key, we know our students well enough to make it. "Do this so you can get a good job someday" holds little allure for a seven-year-old. "Do this and it will improve your game score" might be more enticing.

Habits of Mind

The work on habits of mind by Arthur Costa and Bena Kallick (2000) has huge implications for teaching. In addition to the content of lessons,

Reading and Writing Mini-lesson Content	Social Studies Content Connection	Science Content Connection	Sample Nonfiction Texts, Not Including Assigned Textbooks
Understanding of genre	Reading or writing editorial, opinion for or against an issue or historical personage, persuasive, list of facts, reading between the lines	Reading or writing factual information, discerning what information may be omitted, recognizing story as science, feature article, editorial, opinion	
Use of literary devices	Noticing how use of language, metaphor, allusion, comparison, foreshadowing affect understanding of social studies content	Noticing how use of language and metaphor helps in understanding technical terms	
Use of story elements	Recognizing setting, mood, tone, plot, and character with social studies readings and/or using these for writing in social studies	Recognizing importance of setting, plot, and movement through time in science readings and using these in science writing; learning facts through story	
Accessing previous knowledge	Spiraling back to recall previous knowledge: What do we know about this from last year's content? What do we know from our own experience? What do we know from other texts we've read? How does this sound familiar? How is it foreign to us?	Practicing bringing forward previous knowledge and experience, including television, to understand current study and facts	
Understanding text features in nonfiction	Use of heading and subheadings, charts, graphs, photos, quotes, maps, words and terms defined in parentheses or sidebars	Use of graphs, charts, photos, headings, subheadings, sidebars arrows, diagrams, drawings	

Figure 5–6   *Interconnectedness of reading and writing minilessons with content area instruction*

teachers consider ways to teach students how to live as thinkers. Some of the habits of mind include managing impulsivity, thinking flexibly, using past knowledge, and my personal favorite, appreciating humor. Their list of sixteen habits of mind truly extends teaching beyond the realm of transmitting information or preparing students for state tests. It gives us a North Star view of how great the impact of our teaching can be on students' thinking and their lives. During a lesson, we can consider how we are modeling, or directly teaching, each of the sixteen habits. I recommend reading Costa and Kallick's work. They have published several texts that examine the habits of mind and how to teach them in depth.

I would like to boldly add another habit of mind to Costa and Kallick's list: *revision*. Revision is a way to live—the thinking, creative human expects and welcomes revision. Coaching and encouraging students to revise their thinking, their initial statements, their writing, and so on should not indicate that something is amiss, but rather that the thinking person reconsiders and deepens his work, his life, and his thought. Teachers (and writing consultants) must be willing to revise also.

Qualities of Good Reading and Writing

When we design any unit of study in reading and writing (and in content areas), we need to keep in mind foundational core learning. It is true that there is so much to teach. But as we saw earlier, teachers must consider whether the content of a lesson is actually worth the time. I like to point teachers toward the qualities of good reading and writing as one way to measure the long-lasting value of a lesson or group of lessons. This means that every lesson should have at its center a quality of good reading or writing. Let's look at some of these qualities. Qualities of good reading and writing are behaviors and strategies that readers use to access and comprehend texts. They include the following.

- organization

- solid ideas with support

- word choice

- use of conventions

- genre

- voice

Imagine that you want to teach a lesson on character traits. Where does it fit in the preceding list of qualities? It appears to fit into several categories, including understanding genre (some genres lend themselves to certain types of characters), solid ideas with support (character traits are often the support for the ideas in the text), and possibly voice, depending on whether it is a first-person narrative or written with a clear and distinct voice. Thinking about each of these possibilities confirms that work on character traits will improve students' work not only as readers, but as writers. It may also spill over into their content area work, making it a very strong series of minilessons. In any case, you will want to circle back to it as often as possible to reinforce and practice with students this important work.

Let's actually look at the list of qualities of good reading and writing as a framework for planning lessons. In each unit of study, teachers could consider each quality within the genre or content to be taught. For example, in a unit of study on nonfiction reading and writing, we could teach organizing nonfiction writing and/or using organization to access information from a text as a reader. We could consider word choice: which types of words help us write well in nonfiction, which specialized words we need, and which words make all writing lively and interesting, such as strong verbs and nouns. Obviously, conventions are critical to extracting meaning from any text. But which conventions are most visible in nonfiction? These questions help teachers think about anchoring every unit of study in a meaningful foundation.

Making Time in a Minilesson to Give Gracious Support to All Learners

Imagine this. You are in a classroom during a minilesson, and students raise their hands to respond to the teacher's question. She points to one student whose hand is raised. He immediately turns red, giggles, drops his head, and mumbles, "I forgot what I was going to say." How does the teacher respond to this young learner? Does she call on someone else? Does she wait for the student to respond? Does she give him the opportunity to recall the idea he surely had in his mind, believing that he does have something he to say if he can only get the words out?

How the teacher responds gives students a clear message. They know all our intentions from watching what we do and how we react. Is the teacher the focal point of the classroom? Then the "right answer" is most important to the teacher. Is time too important to waste on a student finding his voice? Then some students may never find theirs. Is a student told not to raise his hand unless he has something to say? Then he's learned not to take risks and not to trust the process of new thinking. Imagine a dinner conversation where someone is told to not participate if he can't remember what he wants to say! We teach students much by the way we respond to their attempts, approximations, and risks.

We all know how easy it is to lean on the students who are quick to respond. We ask a few questions, they seem to know and offer the answers, and we assume—or hope—that the others are with us too. But all students suffer in this case. The quick ones learn to shoulder too much of the talk and learning in the room, and perhaps they lose respect for others; the quiet ones learn they have little to say or that it's safer to say little. Either way, they are not performing their best.

Fourth graders in Alison Meiseles' class know they can trust the community and their teacher enough to share their thinking, even when it is new and untried, or different, or still fuzzy. Alison gently, but energetically, supports her students by listening, talking, coaching, reminding, and encouraging them. She reminds them of all they know already. She points to charts they have made together. She gives them chances to process with partners. And she gives them time.

On the day I visit, they are just finishing a literary essay unit of study. Alison is teaching a minilesson on writing a concluding paragraph and demonstrating that it is not hard to do if you have been thinking, reflecting, and revising all along. One student raises his hand to ask a question, and then forgets what he wanted to ask. Instead of moving on, Alison says, "OK, I'm going to rewind and throw back to you what I was saying. Maybe that will help you remember." She pretends to throw a ball at the student while repeating her last sentence, and the boy breaks out into a smile and asks his question. The few seconds it took to do this showed how much she cares for each learner. Every question matters; every thought counts.

Yes, yes, I know that minilessons are supposed to be short! I know that we don't have time to entertain every remark and question. But Alison knows her students so well—as do most good teachers—that she knows how and when to include their questions in her lesson. She also sets aside processing time when she listens to partners talk so she can anticipate trouble and address it immediately. She assigns partners very carefully so that students are matched by individual strengths they bring to a partnership, not by ability grouping. An academically advanced student may be paired with one who is patient and kind—they have perspectives that inform each other.

Good teachers like Alison have a vision for all learners and a sense of how they fit within the content of each minilesson. They provide time and space for everyone, and they are diligent about visiting students during processing time. They allow wait time before filling in answers. They rewind and reteach, if necessary. They scaffold to support and encourage. They know they teach the whole child, not just the content. Their students matter more than scores and deadlines.

Summary

As we desire to become better and more professional teachers, we take time to examine our work closely, carefully, and critically. We never undermine teachers' learning by being mean or disparaging to others (after all, we wouldn't do that to children). But we remain open to studying teaching and to questioning whether it is thorough, deep, and long-lasting. The best test is to look at student work, for that will clearly show the state of the class's learning and the quality of our teaching. We no longer rest on "I taught it, but she didn't learn it." If students haven't learned what we've taught, we must examine out teaching and teach it again.

For teachers to do

- Look over planned minilessons to organize them as theme and development or theme and variation; if no connecting thread exists between all the lessons, reconsider your rationale for teaching them.

- Study past lessons to determine how you could group them better in the future or for the next year.

- Study student work across ability levels to see if there is a direct correlation between your teaching and student work.

- Use this to reflect on where your teaching may need to change.

- Plan lessons across content areas that reflect work in reading and writing workshop and vice versa.

- Incorporate habits of mind and qualities of good reading and writing into your teaching and into your daily interactions with students.

- Make time for students in your lessons.

Other Daily Types of Whole-Class Teaching

Workshop Share Time, Morning Meeting, Read-Aloud, Celebrations

In any classroom, there are multiple occasions for students to come to-gether as a whole group during the day. The nature of teaching is gath-ering students together for varying reasons—to begin an inquiry, to give instructions, to reteach, review, or reflect. Perhaps we must relay im-portant information, such as a change in schedule, or we gather to muse on their not-so-quick exit in the last fire drill, or to discuss ways to help the class work more efficiently. Of course, in self-contained classrooms, we gather for instruction in other content areas. Although the minilesson is very efficient workshop teaching, it would be shortsighted to claim that it is the only whole-class teaching we do.

In this chapter we will look at other ways we teach students as a whole group. Throughout the day, instruction takes place in how we begin and end the day, ways we process the end of each session of reading and writ-ing, how we frame and use read-aloud time, and how we celebrate learning together. Students learn from everything that happens in a classroom. We must not neglect other opportunities for instruction across the day, nor must we think that minilessons teach them everything they need to know. We will look at whole-class teaching in the following containers.

◈ end-of-workshop share sessions

◈ morning meetings

◈ read-aloud time

◈ celebrations

End-of-Workshop Share Sessions

Once a month I meet with my spiritual director. She is a great listener, but usually I begin by saying that I have nothing to share. However, after a few moments of her patient, gentle waiting, I hear myself say things that reveal deep inner workings of my spirit and mind. I know that speaking aloud helps these ideas and feelings gel in my mind and heart. Knowing I have time to share helps me live toward the conversations I have with her.

Workshop share time is certainly not spiritual direction. But it is a time for revealing conversation, that is, thoughtful speaking and listening. This conversation comes at the end of the workshop, after the minilesson, the small-group work, and conferring. It signals the closure of the day's workshop, the ending or final benediction on the work. However, share time (often called "the share" or share session) not only is the dismissal but is a second teaching time or a processing time (Calkins et al. 2003). Used thoughtfully, it contributes to the working and wisdom of writing workshop. We send students off from workshop feeling satisfied with their work and thinking about more they could do.

In her lovely book *Don't Forget to Share: The Crucial Last Step in the Writing Workshop*, Leah Mermelstein (2007) describes several types of shares. These include sharing the content (33), craft decisions (46), process (59), and progress (69). In each case, the share session elevates student learning. Students leave the share with more work to do or an intellectually provocative point to ponder.

What's the Purpose of Sharing?

Two of my mentors, Lucy Calkins and Isoke Nia, asked me this question so many times that their voices resound inside my head whenever I am teaching or planning to teach: *What is your purpose? What is your purpose?* Carl Anderson, my staff developer and author of *How's It Going?* (2000) and *Assessing Writers* (2005), still says to me, "If you don't know why you are doing it, don't do it."

So it is with the share session at the end of workshop teaching. If we don't know why we are doing it, or if our intention is merely to showcase certain students' work, then the *purpose* does not justify the time spent.

I emphasize that a share session is short. It takes no more than three to five minutes. Still, even five minutes not used to its best effect adds up to hours wasted over the course of a year. The share is worthy of its five minutes, and with careful thought and planning, is an important whole-class "bookend" to the minilesson. If we think of it as such—that is, supporting the reading or writing time with minilesson on one side and share on the other—then the significance of the share is clear. Measuring share time against the minilesson also raises the bar for what we expect it to accomplish.

As with all short instruction, there is little time to waste in share sessions. Students come back to the teaching area quickly for sharing or can remain at their seats and turn to one direction. Just like routines for minilessons, this must be rehearsed. It helps to have a cue that writing or reading time is drawing to a close, such as a bell, music, a signal, phrase, or soft gong. Give students two to three minutes to finish up their work, and then repeat the bell, or strike the gong softly twice, to cue students to regather for sharing.

The share session may recall the minilesson, and students may refer to how their work has gone—mostly focusing on the process, not the product. This means that students will rarely sit in an author's chair and read their writing aloud during share sessions. They may talk about how the minilesson has helped their independent work, or their plans for trying it again the next day, or that they used strategies from previous minilessons today. They may read a short excerpt from writing where they demonstrate how the minilesson helped them clarify or revise. Although the teacher does not exclusively own the share, he may shape it, either by deciding which students will share based on observations from conferring or small-group work or by sharing his own assessment of the work of the day. This means the teacher uses the share session to push or sculpt student learning.

Content of share sessions differs and might include one or more of the following from the teacher's point of view.

- successes and surprises

- how hard or easy it was to do the work

- observation of new understandings emerging

- application to previous minilessons

- the need for reteaching

- the need for more student practice of the strategy

- how the strategy connects to additional work across the day, including content area applications

- teacher observations from small groups and conferences

◈ possibilities for ongoing practice, the next minilesson, or homework

In addition, the share time provides closure to the workshop time. Closure is not: "OK, put away your writing and let's get ready for lunch." This destroys the dignity of the work and communicates that we read or write around an imposed schedule that dictates when to begin and end. Of course, as teachers, we know that in many ways that is true, and we understand why this is necessary in schools. But we hope students have more sense of the "sacredness" of time and space to read and write and learn, and the share session as *closure* provides this.

Share sessions give students time to discuss, to process, and to reflect on their work. In a safe environment, students can say that the strategy was hard, and their classmates will understand. They can share successes or their novice attempts at a strategy. Time for making connections and plans, self-evaluation, and self-assignment are built into their share work. Although they cannot consider every point every day, lest they simply check off items on a list, some coaching is helpful to give students ideas for what they could share (Figure 6–1). Though each student will not share with the class every day, the habit of reflection is important for learning.

Today, how did I . . .

❑ use the minilesson strategy in my reading or writing?

❑ revise or reread?

❑ work with my partner?

❑ use my notebook as a tool for learning?

❑ use a mentor text?

❑ choose words carefully or work on other qualities of good writing?

❑ apply my thinking?

❑ revisit previous minilessons?

❑ assign myself work?

❑ work through difficulty?

❑ work automatically on a strategy I learned earlier?

Figure 6–1   *Phrases to help students reflect on work in preparation for sharing*

Occasionally, you might ask students to write their share session ideas on sticky notes or index cards for you to read later. This helps students to feel their reflections, questions, or problems are all given attention, even though only two or three students will speak aloud in a daily share session.

Because the share session is not an "on the fly" meeting, teachers must orchestrate it. Although I recommend that you remain open to surprise, it helps to have some ideas for possible shares (Figure 6–2). You will notice that many of the share introductions in Figure 6–2 require the teacher to have figured out the share content during the writing time. Although you may have something in mind that you hope students will share, most likely the share will arise from the work during writing time. Often it is related to the minilesson, but this is not necessary. What is necessary is that it contain information that all students may find useful either at that moment or at a later time and that it prepare the way for additional reading or writing.

❑ Today (student's name) and I discovered something during a conference and he (or she) has given me permission to share our thinking with you (or he or she would like to share it with you)

❑ I noticed that three students outgrew my minilesson with their smart thinking. They've agreed to tell you about what they did.

❑ Today a small group asked if they could connect today's minilesson with something we did in social studies a few weeks ago. They want to share their idea with you.

❑ I know that the strategy from today's minilesson was difficult, but three students want to tell you how they worked through that difficulty.

❑ Sometimes we all struggle to understand a new concept. Today Mary wants to talk to you about how it feels to struggle and what she plans to do about it.

❑ When we learn something new, it often helps us to think about where it fits in with our previous learning. Lisa and Joseph want to tell you about how today's revision strategy fits in with some revision they did in the last unit of study.

❑ It is so exciting when we have a breakthrough what we are trying to do as writers (or readers). Anthony was working hard to get the dialogue in his narrative to sound authentic, and he is going to tell you how today's minilesson helped him do that.

Figure 6–2 *Possible language for teachers to use in orchestrating share sessions*

For teachers, share time is a great gift. We hear student voices honestly speaking their triumphs and struggles. We get to highlight new thinking and fascinating breakthroughs in understanding that we know happen every day. We use the work of all students to inform the others. And we set aside a time for daily minicelebration of the hard and joyful work that is literacy learning.

Morning Meetings

Once again I am visiting Sarah Daunis' classroom. I have arrived early enough to be part of their morning meeting, and students scoot over on a bench to make room for me. They are sending morning greetings around the circle, and at my turn, I follow their lead and stand up to bow and say good morning to my neighbor. Students smile at my dramatic greeting and make eye contact with each other to pass the greeting along. I feel part of a humane and welcoming way to begin the day.

Morning meeting is a ritual in many classrooms. More than the first academic event of the day, morning meeting is whole-class teaching about ways to build respect and trust, to gain social graces, and to enjoy acceptance as part of the group. Roxane Kriete (2002, 8) says, "Its mixture of routine and surprise, of comfort and challenge, make morning meeting a treasured and flexible teaching tool." Morning meeting gives students a sense of significance—all students are important members of the class—and respects children's need to have fun. It teaches students how to take care of each other, how to speak clearly and listen carefully, and how to build vocabulary to share their tragedies, joys, cares, and concerns.

What type of actual "teaching" occurs in morning meeting? Aside from ways to act and speak and the workings of social niceties, how does morning meeting contribute to the academic knowledge of young learners?

First, I believe that the social and emotional components of morning meeting rituals are justification for including it in the day's work. We teach students how to act when we model it and explicitly provide language to use and choices to make in various situations. Although I am not advocating a return to nineteenth-century finishing schools, it is true that young people often come to school without social behaviors that will make life smoother for them. And if they don't learn this at home, it is our joy to teach them—with respect and with dignity. Following is a list of socially savvy student learning from morning meetings.

- how to greet a latecomer with compassion and acceptance

- how to comfort someone who is sad or embarrassed

- how to filter out words that could be offensive to others

- how to greet a new acquaintance or business partner

- how to ask someone his or her name if you've forgotten it

- how to inquire as to a person's health or family

- how to begin a conversation and how to keep it going

- how to include a quiet person in conversation

- how to respond to others politely

- how to agree to disagree

- how to disagree with dignity and grace

- how to monitor a conversation to be sure you are not monopolizing it

- how to show interest in another's distress; express empathy

Notice that the preceding "social graces" end up supporting academic work. Students who can talk easily with each other are more likely to have successful partner and group conversations about books, writing, or content information. They are more likely to stay on topic in conversation. And they are more likely to get along in and out of school, leaving more time for teaching and learning rather than monitoring their behavior.

Often teachers use morning meeting simply to name the weather, count the school days, and go over the schedule for the day. Certainly these are acceptable items to include in morning meeting, but a meeting to build deep social relationships and conversational skills needs more than enumeration of daily facts. Use morning meeting to share school news and ask students to share news from their lives, even if it is seemingly insignificant "news," such as "My little brother spit out his cereal at me this morning." What children choose to share about themselves is often a window into who they are and what they are thinking. Use morning meeting to air and discuss challenges the class is facing, for example, "Some class members are feeling uncomfortable with the way their personal belongings are treated when others go to the clothing closet. Let's talk about how we can change that." And morning meeting can also be a time to discuss plans and hopes. For example, "We all hope to be able to make the class library more useful for everyone. Let's think together on ways we can manage that." Morning meeting contributes to the sense of community, the belief in the ability of all to solve problems and share triumphs and shortcomings, and the creation of wise and wonderful intellectual friendships.

Morning meeting also contributes directly to academic skills. By teaching learners to share and listen to each other's concerns, morning meeting builds an *academic atmosphere* of trust and mutual investment in each other's learning. For example, let's imagine a doctoral studies cohort meeting together on retreat to network, plan, and discuss various research projects. Pretty advanced work, eh? But elementary students are doing this—on their level, of course—when they meet together in morning meeting. In an excerpt from a morning meeting transcript in a fourth-grade classroom that I studied, I noticed how many of the interactions signal the same kind of thinking work that our hypothetical doctoral cohort group might practice.

- A student introduces her topic/issue and says as much or as little about it as the group needs in order to understand—no wasted words.

- The group is asked to consider the issue at hand, and invited to ask questions; the student expects that the group can and will help or at least be interested and compassionate.

- The group asks questions that probe the student's thinking; questions are carefully shaped.

- There is a period of musing, reference to previous conversations, and making connections.

- The moderator may need to keep participants on track as expansive thinking can sometimes lead far away from the topic.

- The group makes suggestions for further investigation or comments about different ways to view the issue.

- The student graciously accepts these offerings and considers whether they will help her.

- Another person in the group continues.

In this group, there is ritual, comfort, and expectation—expectation that something good will happen and expectation that everyone is capable of contributing to the group. We all are smart and creative. We collaborate to create learning and to create this community. We discuss problems openly, and often talking aloud makes a solution appear. There is group identity. The group works to learn to compose good questions and to keep attention on the person speaking and/or the problem at hand. One person's difficulty or joys are shared by all. We engage with someone else's thinking and practice controlling rambling thoughts or inattention. We take turns having the chair. We think through others' ideas with them. It sounds like a doctoral cohort meeting to me!

Morning meeting teaches habits of mind (Sizer 1992; Costa and Kallick 2000; Costa 2001; Carter et al. 2006) that spill into the academic studies of the day: inquiry, creative thinking, problem solving, expansive thinking, applying learning to one's situation, patience, focus and clarity, building respect for everyone's thinking.

Read-Aloud Time

Surely many of us recall the comfort of reading and rereading a special book with someone we love, whether a parent who read to us years ago or a grandchild to whom we read today. Those who have not had this experience somehow know they have missed something special. Reading aloud is joy, calm, and rest. It is excitement, intellectual challenge, and creative stimulation (Hoyt 2006; Hahn 2002; Fox 2001). No wonder we listen to audio books in our cars on the way to work or on long trips—in our adult world, it is the closest we get to recapturing read-aloud time.

I believe that reading aloud to students is the single most important event of the school day and the most effective model for literacy learning (Serafini and Giordis 2003). Reading aloud must happen every day, in every grade, and across genres (Laminack and Wadsworth 2006a). There is no excuse for omitting it. It is just too essential for all students and for our teaching.

When we read aloud, we call students to a common literacy experience. We gather around—on rugs, on benches, on pillows—and we grow together in our understanding of life through the worlds and words of stories. Throughout history, authors have struggled to explore the "human condition" in their stories, essays, and poems. When we read aloud, we show students that their problems and joys are universal and that we are all the same in more ways than we realize. How can we hate when we all suffer and rejoice and share others' hearts through books? Reading aloud calls us to be our most human, to have more of ourselves through the stories we share and love.

A rich read-aloud life means more to students than quiet time for relaxing or nodding off. Smart teachers use read-aloud time to build community and to establish a few mentor texts from which to teach many skills in reading and writing (Ray 2000, 2002). They also demonstrate literate thinking by "thinking aloud" for students (Ray 2000; Wilhelm 2001; Angelillo 2003). We teach them the lifelong habit of snuggling up with a good book and rereading a much-loved text and how to think beyond plot to consider big ideas.

When we read aloud, we model the literate life in its simplest to its most sophisticated form. Notice the increasing complexity of the list in Figure 6–3. We can enjoy a good story, but as we read it again (and again), we see much more inside it. Although teachers may feel they must regale students with new stories every day, returning to a familiar text builds literary vision. Similarly, secondary teachers will find a wealth of literary concepts to teach in well-written picture books.

I cannot overemphasize how important it is for students to hear us read, to hear us roll language around and play with the music of a phrase,

❑ to provide enjoyment

❑ to model the love of books

❑ to model how reading sounds

❑ to model finding one's self inside another's story

❑ to build community and trust

❑ to provide shared experience and common texts

❑ to begin classroom discussion

❑ to explore crises or difficulties in the classroom

❑ to create a foundational text list from which to draw connections and comparisons

❑ to begin to know a text well

❑ to explore rereading

❑ to introduce and revisit texts to be used for instruction in reading and writing

❑ to explore universal themes

Figure 6–3 *Reading aloud purposes and teaching arranged from simple to sophisticated*

to take on the voice of a character, and, sometimes, to cry during a book. When my son was in high school, I recall being a little worried about how Shakespeare would be taught in his school. I went to his room one night and asked how he was doing with his Shakespeare reading. He answered, "No problem, Mom. Don't you remember that when we were little, you used to read us the King James Bible every night before bed? So it sounds just like regular talking to me. Now . . . get thee gone from my chambers!"

Obviously I am *not* suggesting that you read Shakespeare or the King James Bible to children, but this does indicate that students pick up language from our reading aloud—yes, even when we think they are asleep!

Using Picture Books to Strengthen Teaching in All Grades

Recently I began rereading many children's books on my shelf. My husband has decided that we have too many books for the floors in our house to support, and so if a new book comes in, an old one must go out. Sigh. I've been rereading old picture books, and I find I can't part with them. This makes me think about rediscovering "old" books. I worry that teachers fear they cannot teach writing workshop because they do not have the latest children's books and cannot afford to buy them. But as I reread fifty-year-old books from my bookshelves, I'm finding that each one of them is a delight, though the illustrations may be less gorgeous than those in recent books. But a great story is a great story, and that is really what matters (Hall 2001; Tiedt 2000; Pearson 2005; Heitmen 2004; Ray 1999).

I brought *Harry the Dirty Dog* by Gene Zion (1956) with me to read aloud to teachers in Indiana recently. In what seems like a simple, almost simplistic text, we found so many points to discuss that teachers from pre-K to college said they would use the book in their classrooms. The point is not that you should use this book—it is only to emphasize that any good book can be a marvelous teaching tool if you only have eyes to see how to use it. Following, I've listed some of the noticings we found in *Harry the Dirty Dog*.

◈ Harry hates to take a bath: Many stories begin with the character becoming discontented and leaving home.

◈ Harry takes matters into his own hands: Part of growing up is beginning to take charge of one's life.

◈ Harry runs away: Many of us are unhappy with something we have to do—how do we hide from it?

- Harry buries the brush: An object can be a focal point in a story—what is the object that causes upheaval in our lives?

- Harry gets dirty and completely changes his identity so that his family can't recognize him: Which new identities do we try on as we grow up? Do we sometimes become unrecognizable to those who know us?

- Harry finds the solution to his problem by digging up the brush: Good characters solve their problems themselves.

We also noticed many writing and reading strategies to teach from the book: beginning with action, introducing the problem early in the story, building suspense, using punctuation to shape meaning, use of superlatives, dialogue that moves the story, a distinct point where the story "turns," sparse description that is critical to understanding. We also found universal themes: family relationships, the comfort of home, coming of age, and the grass is always greener on the other side of the fence (OK, sometimes it really is greener there!). Again, all this demonstrates that even a simple text can yield many lessons on many levels if chosen and used carefully. After our day studying *Harry*, I know teachers will never think of that book the same way nor will their read-alouds ever be shallow again.

When we read aloud, we should follow several guidelines. Never read aloud a book you have not read yourself—it is not professional nor best practice to "want to find out the ending with the students." You cannot teach what you don't know. Read the book first several times and decide if it is appropriate for your students.

Do not confuse reading aloud with shared reading. Students do not have the text before them during a read-aloud; if they do, it is technically a shared read. Shared reading has many benefits, but it is not the same as reading aloud. Choose a comfortable place for the read-aloud session, and plan to leave the book available for students to revisit at another time. Keep a chart of read-alouds you've done. Go back and make a separate chart for each read-aloud as it becomes a mentor text. Indicate how students can use it as readers and writers. Teach students to use the chart to support their reading and writing.

Some read-aloud texts will not become mentor texts for your class. You may read them a few times and enjoy them, but the class may not fall in love. One class may love, another may be lukewarm. Trust your students and yourself. It pays to use only texts they love for mentor texts, though you should feel free to read many kinds of text to them. Or you may choose to read aloud a novel, and only portions of it, as mentor texts for students.

Celebrations

Although we know that celebrating reading and writing is a regular part of workshop classrooms, we often don't think of celebrations as "whole-class teaching." In some unfortunate cases, celebrations become more about who's pouring out the lemonade and who's monitoring the noise level. But celebrations are teaching opportunities. Planned for the end of a writing cycle or unit of study, a celebration marks writing publication or recognition of reading learning in a regular, predictable fashion. Celebrations can be dignified and joyous. And they can be occasions for teaching students polite ways to respond to each other and to evaluate their own work with honesty and pride.

A celebration should be fun, building community with a shared event and with the excitement and anticipation of an upcoming holiday. A celebration solidifies one's membership in the community and one's identity as a reader and writer. It can be a social event when others—administrators, literacy coaches, other classes or school staff, and of course, parents—are invited to join the community's celebration. Or it can be an intimate sharing just among class members, a quiet, meaningful appreciation of each other's hopes and work. We admire and rejoice in others' successes, even if we are not part of them. Students learn that we recognize and value the steps on the learning journey by celebrating. We take time to congratulate ourselves on what we've accomplished and look forward to what we hope to accomplish next.

Teachers can use the celebration to build in reflection. For example, the next day's morning meeting could contain a discussion on how smoothly the celebration itself went, with language such as, "Wasn't that a wonderful celebration we had yesterday?" "My favorite part was when we all clapped and hooted at the end." "Do you remember when Don read his best paragraph and we cried?" In real life, we all look back and relive celebrations—"Wasn't the food at that wedding reception just scrumptious?" "Wasn't Jenny's story hilarious?"—with fondness and amazement. Teach students that looking back to recall the celebrations is part of the fun and the benefit of them. And when we find ourselves in a time of trouble, we can live off a celebration for a long time.

Celebration should include instruction on ways to respond to others' work, with additional teaching taking place each time the class celebrates (Figure 6-4). Responses should always indicate recognition of the learning another student did. Students can evaluate which types of responses to their work were helpful, and request other kinds of responses they would like to get. Mostly, students need to know that with celebration comes looking back and looking forward—what did we do that was wonderful, what did we learn, and where do we need to do more work?

Celebration and Self-Evaluation for Students

Because we hope students will take ownership of their learning by assessing their work, celebrations are the perfect opportunity for teaching them

---

❏ I liked the way you added to the sentence you shared, especially because I know you've been working so hard on writing longer sentences.

❏ Your ending was surprising. It shows you really worked on avoiding dull endings.

❏ I really could see your attention to craft in your writing, especially where your used lots of alliteration.

❏ I'm happy that you seem to have really "gotten" how to write dialogue, even though I am still trying to figure it out

❏ Your mentor text really shows through, especially in the part where you built suspense

❏ I see you decided to use what we talked about in our partnership, and that encourages me to use partnership time more usefully

❏ I could see the qualities of good writing in your piece, and it tells me that you really paid attention as a writer

❏ You must have done some very smart revisions, because your piece is so good now

❏ Your voice really showed in your writing as if I could hear you reading it to me

❏ The way you had your two characters yell at each other gave me an idea for revising the relationship between the two characters in my story.

Figure 6-4   *Ways for students to respond orally and/or in writing to others' sharing during a celebration*

to do this. By learning to stop and think about their work and trying to be objective (yes, I know how hard this is!), students learn a great lesson about how to navigate their learning. During the celebration, students might take notes on the comments other students give them, or they could read over written comment sheets and respond back to them. Although I don't think students need to answer every question every time, following are some questions students might use to begin to assess their own work.

* Does this writing show my best capability? Did I give it my best?

* Where are two places where I made a craft move I am proud of?

* Where is my best revision and why?

* Where did I use conventions deliberately to make meaning?

* Where is one place in my writing that I think I could have done better?

* How can I make plans to study something I have trouble doing, such as writing good beginnings?

* What can I assign to myself for more learning or for an independent project?

* Which mentor text did I use and how does it show up in my writing?

* Where is the evidence of several minilessons in my work?

* Where is evidence of attention to qualities of good writing?

* Where is evidence of carrying forward previous learning to this unit?

* What is the most interesting thing I learned from my writing in this unit?

Celebration and Self-Evaluation for Teachers

Any course of study is successful only to the extent that we, as teachers, make plans to implement what we have learned about teaching and our students' progress. Therefore, we can use the occasion of a class celebration to evaluate student work as a mirror of our own work.

- Celebrate your learning by sharing a short selection of your writing with students in a *risk-free* way. Become part of the celebration.

- Assess your own learning: which parts of the process seem intuitive and which seem more difficult to grasp? How can you "take on" the harder parts to master them, that is, lean into the gaps to stretch our thinking and learning? What plans can you make for further learning or investigation?

- Name one part of the unit of study that you will try to improve before repeating the unit the next year. How will you use student writing to inform your teaching? How will you use your own writing to inform teaching? What professional literature might you seek out to inform your work?

- Write the titles of two to three children's texts that you might use the next year as mentor texts. Evaluate the effectiveness of the mentor texts you used this time.

- Working with other teachers in the same grade, evaluate at least three minilessons *in depth* that you did in the unit. Include how well you think the lessons worked, how they helped students, and how the lessons fit together as a teaching thread.

- Rejoice!

Teachers need time to reflect. If there are team meetings, these could be spent reflecting at the end of units, while backward planning (Wiggins and McTighe 2005) for the next unit. Breakfast meetings are possible, as is self-reflection at the end of the celebration day along with the students. Perhaps teachers can study several samples of student work at the end of each unit by writing thoughts on how their teaching is shown in student work and plans for future work.

Some possible questions for teachers to ask at the end of a study

- Based on my backward planning, how well did individual students learn the skills of this unit?

- How did I use assessment to plan instruction and how effective was this?

- How did I differentiate instruction to meet the needs of students and was this successful?

- Which skills do I need to reteach and to which students?

- How would I have taught certain minilessons differently and why?

- How will I work on transfer of skills from this unit to the next?

- What will I do differently the next time?

- Does my teaching show clearly in students' work?

Types of Celebrations

Just as there are many types of celebrations in our outside lives, there should be a variety of celebrations in classrooms. Repeating a type of celebration again and again may make it familiar, but may also make it boring. We want to balance ritual and expectation with spontaneity and creativity. If every party were a wedding celebration, we'd be tired of them after awhile. On the other hand, it's comforting to know that every Thanksgiving dinner serves up a turkey—however overdone and dry. It's a constant that we expect and love. Variety and constancy should be sewn into each celebration.

Let's start with simple rituals that might remain constant. Each of these is your choice, of course. This list is a gathering of suggestions, not a mandated celebration curriculum! But each item on the list is easy enough to continue each time without affecting the content of the celebration—it is like the turkey part of Thanksgiving or the obligatory toast at a wedding reception. This gives students as sense of "we know how celebrations go" even when the type of each celebration will differ.

- We have our celebrations at the same time, for example, on the last Friday morning the month, except when holidays interfere and we have to reschedule.

- We always send each other invitations; each student sends an invitation to one other student in the class.

- We find some way to "dress up" for the day, which may range from everyone wearing sneakers, putting red ribbons around our wrists, or wearing pajamas (check with your administrators about this one first!); be sure this is an easy dress-up ritual that all can fulfill without feeling marginalized.

- ◈ We rearrange the furniture and/or dim the lights; perhaps we light an electric candle (such as holiday window lights that use a single six-watt bulb).

- ◈ We play music softly in the background.

- ◈ We always have juice afterward.

- ◈ We spend the rest of the morning reading, or we go to the library, or we write to someone to describe our celebration.

On the other hand, parts of celebration will differ. For one thing, the content will obviously change—are we sharing poetry, notebook entries, revisions we are proud of, our editorials, book reviews, and so on? The method of sharing will differ with some of the suggestions below. Again, this is not the definitive list of sharing possibilities, nor is it the curriculum for sharing from on high. Use your judgment and creativity, and ask your students to join you in making decisions.

- ◈ We sit in a circle and wait for silence to read aloud our favorite sentence or two. Each person's reading is followed by fifteen to thirty seconds of silence so the group can contemplate it before the next person reads. There are no comments during this performance—students wait till the end to give feedback to each other. The teacher may tape their readings and make a transcript of the "poem" they create from it. This can be distributed to all students.

- ◈ We sit at a table other than our regular table and read one or two paragraphs from our writing. Members of the new group give feedback; the reader/writer may ask them to listen for a specific item, such as, "Please listen to the way I tried to tell the inner story of my character."

- ◈ We leave our writing on our tables and we move around, sitting in different chairs to read what others have written. Beside each writing piece is a comment sheet, and we sign our names and write comments before moving on to the next empty seat. This is done in silence, except for quiet music. It can go on for thirty minutes or until students begin to tire.

- Students share at their tables, especially if there are visitors in the room.

- Students share by reading at a podium, choosing only one section to read. This may include "my favorite dialogue, my best revision, my suspense building, my introduction of the problem, my great solution to the problem," and so on.

- Students visit or invite another class into the celebration and share with other students one on one.

Celebrations are a natural part of our lives. We celebrate as families and as communities—and a class is a family as well as a learning community. Throughout life, we mark milestones by coming together to meet or to feast—holidays, religious events, new jobs, promotions, birthdays and births, engagements, weddings. Families and communities come together to support each other and share the good times, and sadly, the bad times too. This makes us stronger, wiser, and with time, more loving and generous with others.

Summary

In addition to minilessons, there are other types of whole-class teaching. In order to make the most of all teaching opportunities, we study how to best use these other teaching times. Morning meeting and celebrations are times for teaching social intelligence and community; share sessions and read-aloud provide opportunities for teaching literate behaviors and to challenge ourselves to more learning. Each of these types of whole-class teaching supports the other. Each is a tool for deep teaching and each has its place in the classroom. It all depends on purpose—what do we hope to accomplish with each type of whole-class teaching? The wise teacher looks across them all to study how his teaching is rich and textured to meet the many needs of all students.

For teachers to do

- Be sure that each type of whole-class teaching is present in your class.

- Examine each type to be sure that you are using it as an opportunity for teaching.

- Choose one type of whole-class teaching to study.

- Make an audiotape of one session and study it.

- Make sure you know the purpose for each lesson and each type of teaching.

- Work to make your teaching deliberate and thorough.

Other Types of Minilessons

Inquiry, Coaching, Demonstration

If we could peek inside classrooms of fabulous teachers, we'd see all kinds of wonderful teaching. We'd see energy and excitement, and we'd see students learning. The science teacher has set up a lab and students are chatting away in an inquiry into how gravity works. The physical education teacher has students playing soccer, and she is coaching them on form and style. A music teacher is demonstrating the correct way to hold a violin bow. A math teacher is reteaching a concept using different manipulatives than he used the first time around. All of these teachers are doing what good teachers do: they use whatever teaching tools they can to provide students with opportunities to experience and learn in powerful, meaningful, and lasting ways.

Although the subject of this chapter may seem to fly in the face of current belief, there is no doubt in my mind that while the formula for a minilesson is a strong and efficient way to teach, it is not the only way to teach. To claim that there is only one way to teach is to ignore the choice and the strength that comes from teachers choosing their methods and best practice. We would not be happy with a carpenter who only used hammers, nor would we approve of a physician who prescribed only one medication. We would quickly get bored if dinner was grilled every night, and wearing the same silk shirt every day gets dingy after awhile. Any good thing, no matter how wonderful it is, can be overused or used inappropriately. We require a variety of foods, and a variety of tools, and a variety of medicines to suit our needs and our health.

And so teachers must have in their teaching toolboxes a variety of teaching structures. Teachers need choice and the freedom to make choices based on professional decision making and knowledge. The wise teacher is flexible and informed.

I must emphasize that the minilesson is an exquisite way to teach. I want all teachers to strive for elegant minilessons. But I also want teachers to be able to shift gears when necessary and teach outside the minilesson box. This is not license to ignore minilessons altogether under the guise of "I've decided I teach better if I talk for forty-five minutes," or even worse, "My students can't 'get it' in only ten minutes." Fortunately, the factory school model is obsolete. Teaching for longer periods of time or teaching in a non-minilesson structure should be *the exception*, not the rule. If we choose not to use a minilesson, we should be able to explain the purpose of choosing another teaching form and how the lesson will be supported by a subsequent return to minilessons.

In this chapter, we'll examine three types of minilesson teaching.

◈ inquiry

◈ demonstration and coaching

◈ extended coaching session

Inquiry

Inquiry-based learning leans heavily on brain research and on the belief that when students discover information on their own, it tends to have more meaning for them. Involving students in exploration and construction of knowledge under the guidance of the teacher allows students to frame and solve problems, to know how to find answers to problems, to persist, and to remove any doubt that they are capable of finding answers. In short, inquiry supports assertive learning.

Inquiry lessons are not quite the same as formal minilessons, though we learn from Lucy Calkins that methods for teaching in minilessons can be explaining and giving an example, guided practice or coaching, and demonstration and inquiry (Calkins, Hartman, and White 2005). So, strictly speaking, an inquiry is a type of minilesson, but it does not follow the traditional minilesson form. To set up and support an inquiry, a teacher must trust that students' findings will be sound. Often in minilessons, teachers know the predicted outcome of the lesson and model for students the skill or strategy they hope students will learn. The teaching point is quite controlled. In inquiry instruction, teachers do not instruct

students on a strategy or some bit of information, but rather on the
method of discovery (Table 7–1). Notice how the same information is

Table 7–1 Comparison Between Traditional Minilesson and Inquiry Lesson

Traditional Minilesson	Inquiry Lesson
Here are the five most important features of a book review.	I've put copies of several book reviews on your tables. Let's read them and try to figure out what the features of the genre are. We'll gather together after twenty minutes to make a chart of our noticings.
You can use strong verbs to make writing exciting.	Let's examine texts to discover which kinds of words make the writing exciting.
You can use semicolons to connect two short sentences and show they have a relationship.	Look through the book you are reading to find semicolons. Then determine why the author used them. We'll talk about what this means for your reading and writing in twenty minutes.
Today we will study one way to organize information in order to write a paragraph.	Let's study these paragraphs to figure out the organizational structure the author used.
Readers can work through a difficult passage by reading it in phrases and accumulating the phrases into sentences.	As you read a difficult passage today, watch what you do to figure out how to get through the difficulty. Notice your thinking as you try to figure something out.
Jane Yolen uses interesting language in her writing, such as alliteration.	Today as you read your Yolen books, notice the kinds of interesting language Jane Yolen uses. We'll regroup to talk about this in twenty minutes.
Today we will look at character traits and how knowing what a character is thinking or feeling helps us to understand a story.	When you read today, use sticky notes to mark places in the text where the writer has told you the character's thoughts or feelings. Think about how this helps you understand and we'll talk about this when we meet together in twenty minutes.

framed differently in traditional minilessons and inquiry lessons. Teachers can choose which lesson is best suited to their purpose. Both types of lessons are important, and teachers should choose each thoughtfully.

As you can see, traditional minilessons are more directed, although for sure they are not "telling" the information but demonstrating and modeling it. In general, the teacher has already determined what students will learn in the minilesson. Inquiry puts the learning and discovery into students' hands. Teachers must be very confident and brave to allow inquiry! But without it, we risk students becoming passive learners. In truth, we want to teach them how to learn and then set them free to do their learning.

When you choose inquiry, keep your purpose in mind. Do you want to teach students a specific strategy by demonstrating or modeling? Or do you want them to figure it out? In the time since I wrote *A Fresh Approach to Teaching Punctuation* (2002), I have visited scores of classrooms where teachers were conducting inquiry into punctuation. In these classes, students are sprawled on the floor with big books or seated at tables with picture books. They read through them to notice the punctuation the authors used and to formulate some understandings of what the author was trying to communicate by using the punctuation marks. In most cases, I hear students delight and laugh. I hear them go beyond what the teacher has requested. I hear them come up with theories about punctuation and then try them out in other texts. I hear conversation and negotiation. I do not hear boredom, resistance, or failure. They all can do it. And they all enjoy doing it. More than anything, students reveal their ability to think, solve problems, reconsider answers, weigh evidence, and revise their ideas. Inquiry brings out their best thinking.

When you decide to have an inquiry lesson in your classroom, keep the following points in mind.

⬧ Make sure students know exactly what they are investigating before they go off.

⬧ Inquiry is noisy and messy, so be patient.

⬧ Be sure you have set up the "experiments," such as choice of text to study, in order to produce some kind of logical and meaningful outcome.

⬧ Visit groups or partners as they work to assess and coach them.

⬧ Allow for originality and creativity in their findings.

- Be sure to process frequently and begin a chart of their findings the same day.

- Clarify students' findings by restating if necessary—ask their permission to do this.

- Make the transfer for students from the inquiry findings to other work in the school.

- Apply their findings to ongoing work in the classroom.

- Encourage students to engage in independent inquiry.

Demonstration and Coaching

When I was still a classroom teacher, Carl Anderson came to my room to teach me and my students how to confer in writing workshop. One day he and I pulled two chairs together in the middle of the room for what he called a "fishbowl," meaning students would be looking in on us as if we were fish on display. As the class watched, Carl conferred with me about my writing. We demonstrated how a conference should look and sound.

This fishbowl, or demonstration, was longer than a usual conference, because as we conferred, we stopped many times to ask my students what they noticed. From this demonstration—which lasted about fifteen to twenty minutes—we made a chart of exactly what happens in a conference, how one behaves in a conference, and how to prepare for a conference. It was a demonstration that my students couldn't forget, because Carl and I played our roles dramatically—and with a good amount of humor. Because it was long, focused on our behaviors and language, and asked students to notice and name what we did and make a chart of expectations together, it was not a traditional minilesson. It did not follow minilesson form, nor did it set out work for students to do that day, unless they happened to confer with us. Nevertheless, it was a crucial lesson in making my workshop successful.

Demonstration is an important type of teaching. Although minilessons usually focus on a strategy for reading or writing, demonstrations usually focus on a way to act or be in workshop. They do not assign students work to do, but rather smooth the way for the work to happen. My workshop would not flow if my students did not know what to expect in a conference, how to respond, and how to prepare for a conference. The demonstration taught students "what I do and why I do it."

Demonstration is akin to "acting" because the teacher and her partner, helper, or another teacher set a scene and then play it through for students. It's like giving students a window into something that ordinarily happens quietly or without fanfare, like a conference, book conversation, or self-monitoring of work.

Let's visit a classroom where the teacher, Sarah, is demonstrating what she does when she thinks she's done. She wants students to see that she has to give herself more work to do and not wait to be assigned more work. Being independent is one way to own learning. Sarah seats herself at the front of the room, and begins the demonstration scene by actually writing in her notebook in front of the class. She looks up and knits her brow, then continues writing. She stops and rereads her writing and appears to correct some spelling. Then she slaps the notebook shut and sighs heavily. "I'm done," she says. Her students giggle.

"No, you aren't," one student calls out.

Sarah looks at him surprised. "I'm not? But I wrote what I wanted to say, and now I have nothing else to do."

Another student calls out. "Go back to your notebook!"

Sarah acts puzzled, and then opens her notebook again. "I guess I can write a new entry," she says. "Hmm . . . and I suppose I can look at my list of possible topics and choose one to write about."

She flips through the pages of her notebook and begins to add to an entry. Then she stops.

"OK, let's freeze," she says. "Let's talk about what you saw."

From her demonstration, students construct a short list of what to do when you think you are finished writing. Sarah continues her demonstration, and over the next fifteen minutes the class makes a solid list of possibilities for independent work (Figure 7–1). Sarah's demonstration has not given them a strategy for writing or reading, nor has she given them an assignment of specific work to do. But she has shown them a way to act and "be" in workshop. From her demonstration they've extracted a list of behaviors that will make their workshop run smoother in future days.

During a demonstration, the teacher stops several times and comes "out of character" to process with students. What do they notice? What behaviors is she demonstrating? How does this apply to their work? What is new, surprising, or confusing about what she is doing? Soliciting responses from students at regular intervals during the performance helps students remember the purpose is to teach a specific behavior, not to get lost in the fun of it. This is also the coaching part of a demonstration lesson:

> ❏ Plan and work on an independent writing project.
>
> ❏ Write in the writer's notebook: a new entry, add to list of topics.
>
> ❏ Look across entries in the notebook to make connections.
>
> ❏ Add on to entries; reflect on entries.
>
> ❏ Work on a list of interesting words.
>
> ❏ Try a new type of notebook entry.
>
> ❏ Reread and revise to practice conventions.
>
> ❏ Study the mentor text.
>
> ❏ Go back to previous writing and revise it with a strategy you just learned.
>
> ❏ Make plans to meet with your partner.
>
> ❏ Decide on the course of your next writing conference.

Figure 7–1   *Possibilities for independent work*

coaching students to name and understand the purpose and teaching point of the demonstration.

Following are some guidelines for planning demonstration lessons.

◈ Demonstrations should present a "scene" of a specific behavior or sets of behaviors you want students to know.

◈ Stop frequently and process the scene with the students.

◈ Engage them to look for specific points, such as "Listen to the language I use as I speak with my partner about her writing."

◈ Make a chart of students' comments as they process the scene.

◈ Rehearse the scene before class so it goes the way you want it to!

◈ Ask students to rehearse, then incorporate what they have seen into their work.

◈ Give students ways to assess their work.

◈ Coach students on how to do what you've demonstrated.

◈ Reinforce student behavior frequently.

I find that students enjoy these demonstration lessons. It gives them a chance to see the teacher "let her hair down." Mostly, it is a clear picture, a movie scene—rather than a "telling"—of what you hope and expect will happen in the class. For many of our visual learners, it is quite helpful in making them part of our literacy club (Smith 1987).

Extended Coaching Session

Fourth-grade teacher Alison has come to teaching from a first career as a television producer. As I watch her teach, I wonder how her previous work has affected what she does. She clearly sees herself as a coach. I see her nudge, support, scaffold, and review with her students. It is an energetic performance that is contagious in its fun and rigor. (See Figure 7–3.)

❏ Fishbowl a conference with another teacher.

❏ Act out a conversation about books or writing.

❏ Demonstrate a behavior in reading or writing workshop, such as becoming independent or asking a partner for help.

❏ Rehearse for a celebration.

❏ Rehearse movement in the room.

❏ Demonstrate how to respond to others in whole-class and small-group conversations.

❏ Show how to act when someone makes you angry or irritated.

❏ Demonstrate how to use the library, when to get the dictionary, and how to care for books.

❏ Show how to keep yourself on task.

❏ Model how to organize yourself for work.

❏ Show what to do when it is hard for you to concentrate.

❏ Act out how partner conversations should sound.

❏ Act out how book club conversations should sound.

❏ Demonstrate words and phrases to use when politely working with others.

Figure 7–2 *Suggestions for demonstration lessons*

Alison's coaching reaches for the highest standard in each student. She shares her observations with them. She recognizes their small (and huge) leaps forward in understanding. She reviews and asks for feedback. She feeds them a bit of information and then stops to process it. She constantly assesses their thinking and growth. She refers back to the text they studied and writing they've done weeks before. She asks for specific recollections of previous lessons. She builds a body of knowledge with the class. And she treats all students with absolute equality. In short, she does what any great coach would do—look for the best in students and challenge them to bring it out.

If you study the transcript, you will see that obviously it is not a minilesson. Alison has determined that in the case of reintroducing writing workshop after a hiatus of a few days and of introducing a new phase of their essay unit of study, her students need more scaffolding and continuous support than a traditional minilesson might provide. This lesson lasted thirty minutes, followed by students going off to write for twenty more minutes. Although the danger in teaching for this length of time is that students will miss your point (and you will lose your grip on the objective), Alison keeps steering her students toward using their "ahas" to create the conclusions to their literary essays.

Alison's lesson was really extended coaching. A coach watches and gives constant feedback, commenting constantly and nudging learners forward. Coaching lessons are the same; the teacher has a vision of what students need to accomplish and through ongoing comment, encouragement, and scaffolding, he pushes students in that direction.

Notice how the teacher did the following during this lesson.

- constant interaction with and encouragement for students; cajoling, supporting, acknowledgment of difficulty

- reference: to previous writing, mentor text, and lessons

- frequent reference to previous charts to make visible the web of learning she has created over time

- willingness to do the work herself

- high expectations for all learners, with respect for those who will share another time

- pulling together many threads in order to make the point of lesson

- validation of student work and thinking aloud

Writers, let's come together. *[invitation to learning]*

Let's bring Janet up to date what we've been doing in writing workshop. And also we've had picnic and "immigration day," so this is a good day to regroup and talk about where we are and where we have to go. *[reorients class and visitor to the ongoing work after interruptions.]*

I've been telling you that literary essay is like Legos, building something slowly and carefully. *[uses a metaphor to deepen understanding of the work]*

Anybody want to build on that. What do you mean by illumination? *[gives students the stage; asks for clarification knowing the student is able to do it]*

So ... let's talk about what you've been doing for me all year starting off with the Langston Hughes poem. We're going to go back to it today. *[recalls previous study of the mentor text and lets class know they need to recall text for today's work]*

I knew that the journey would end up being different, and at times it would be a little difficult, but I gave you my word that all of you are up for the challenge and you are. *[confirms her belief that all students are able to do this writing]*

Most of us are up to drafting and making it into paragraphs. Anyone want to share one more thing before we move on? *[readies class to move on; states what the day's work will be]*

I'm going to keep moving us along. Let's just review this one more time *[points to chart]. [interrupts many questions with decision that chart review will answer most of them]*

What is one thing I make you do at least once a day and not just in writing workshop, but in math, science? Yes! Reflect! In fact, I heard someone came home from a movie with his mom and told her he's going to write a reflection, and I said "I've done my job this year." *[highlights one item from chart she wants students to notice]*

Reflections in my room are not retells. What are they? It's a what? It's an "aha!"—something you never knew before—an awareness. *[redefines an important understanding to scaffold day's lesson]*

I'm going to connect what I just said about reflections and I'm going to add that on to the chart, because today we're going work on writing a summary. *[names the exact teaching for the day after establishing foundational knowledge]*

Remember when I talked about how personal this is to me? When I shared with you that I read this book and I have been studying Langston Hughes since I was in high school? And depending where I am in my life something different is going to be illuminated for me. I read this book when my son was in fourth grade, but it was very different when I read it when he was in tenth grade. Now you all know that my son wants to be ... what? A movie director!! Yes, and I wish he would go for it, but somehow in the back of my mind, I wish he would just be safe and go to college and get a nine-to-five job. What does that remind you of? Hmm, Langston Hughes' father! He wanted him to be an engineer and didn't want him to go off and be a poet. So reading this book this year meant something different to me. So who am I really thinking about? Am I thinking about Langston? No, of course, I'm thinking about my son and about Langston having a similar experience. So I've made a personal connection. *[models her connection so students again hear how to do it]*

So now we're up to the summary. Open your notebooks and look at your early notes. Remember the statement you made early in the study when I met with all of you a few weeks ago? Go back to one you highlighted for me. Everyone have it? *[refers to students' previous work]*

Figure 7–3 *Grade 4 coaching lesson partial transcript with analysis in italics (teacher's words only)*

Let's have a big talk and all share our thoughts. Now that we've read the whole book, does anyone want to just throw out what they're feeling like or another aha they've had after finishing the book? *[opens up discussion]*

Do you want to give me an example of what you just said and how you can connect it to the book itself? *[pushes student to be specific]*

Anybody else? Try to talk about the book. *[nudges students]*

OK, I love where you are going with this. *[validates and nudges]*

I have chills. Does anybody want to build on that? *[validates and nudges]*

OK, I'm going to stop for one second. Would you mind reading for me your aha? *[anchors students back to previous writing]*

Now does that kind of connect? Does it connect to your aha? Was it a little bit deeper and personal? How so? *[pushes student to say what she means]*

So I'm going to just have us look back here on the chart. "It uses the writer's thoughts and personal connections to come to a deeper understanding" (Angelillo 2003). Do you believe yours was deeper? *[asks student for self-assessment]*

So you were talking about how Langston found his voice, but it is also about how over the last five weeks someone else found his voice—you! Do you want to jump in? *[acknowledges student excitement]*

I believe now that your summary is just a really bright version of your aha—the highest light on your aha. Does anyone have any questions because I'm going so above and beyond right now? *[stops to check student understanding of abstract concept]*

Do you know what you just did? You actually used the text to support your metaphor. So you're saying that when you actually analyzed the text, it helped you. *[names what student did]*

It's funny now that you are all raising your hands, but do you remember when you were all so discouraged when we were looking for facts, and you were saying, "I don't know, I don't know." Now how many of you know? *[makes visible student growth in understanding]*

Good, what else? What else? *[expresses excitement in their thinking and hunger for more]*

Do you have something to share? That's OK, you will, you will. *[acknowledges that we all have something to say, but not at the same moment]*

So what are you saying? Are you saying that because he dared to dream, he opened up dreaming for others? Does that trigger something for you? What does that mean for us? *[helps student draw conclusion and make personal connection]*

Let me just stop you for a minute. I love that you used the word *obstacle*. *[congratulates student on vocabulary use]*

Okay, I'm going to engage you. What was it about . . . ? *[feels free to take exception to something a student says]*

Now does that connect? Does it connect to your aha? Was it a little bit deeper and personal? How so? *[helps student to get the personal understanding that he needs in order to write a good conclusion]*

I love the symbolism you just used. I think that shows that you really created new understanding about the text. *[validates student use of metaphor to make meaning from the text]*

Figure 7–3   (Continued)

- respect for how conversations build knowledge

- repeating a student's statement back to clarify

- use of symbolism or metaphor as an acceptable way to explain a difficult concept

- use of challenging vocabulary

Once again, I caution against dismissing the traditional minilesson as the primary mode of teaching. However, in certain circumstances, such as those listed here, teachers may choose to use coaching lessons. Always remember: What is your purpose?

- regrouping after a period of time without writing workshop (holiday, snow days, trips, assemblies)

- beginning a new study with need to situate it in the other work that's been done

- scaffolding of tiny steps toward a new or major understanding

- referring back to many previous texts or writing projects

- building body of knowledge together

- quick assessment of how students are understanding the work

Summary

There are times when teachers need to choose another mode of teaching other than minilessons. Providing their purpose is clear, teachers may decide to conduct an inquiry, coach students into a new skill, or demonstrate by staging a scene. Wise teachers use all the tools in their professional toolboxes, knowing what each tool can accomplish and how to use each tool wisely.

For teachers to do

- Look back over your lessons for a few weeks. Try to determine whether most of them were minilessons. If not, why did you choose another type of lesson? If so, which of the lessons might better have been done better as non-minilessons?

- Ask a colleague to visit your lessons and give you feedback on whether your choice of type of lesson was appropriate.

- Take the same content and imagine it in the various types of lessons. Which seems strongest?

- Make another tape and transcript of a lesson and analyze it to determine what you attempted to do and what you accomplished with each statement you made.

8

Self-Assessment of Whole-Class Teaching

A young man recently sent me his college essay to read. It was skillfully done, with gorgeous words, tension, and use of story as metaphor that was perfect. I told him that I had few suggestions to make, for in truth I find it hardest to confer with someone who writes better than I do. What stuck me most was the young man's incredulity. He wrote to me: Did I really mean it? Was I only trying to make him happy? How could I say it was good when his English teacher hated it? And so on. More than writing a fine essay, I believe this young person needed to develop eyes to see and ears to hear that could help him know when his writing—or anything else—is well done. He needed to work on self-assessment and confidence. He needed to objectively examine his work without others' negative voices jabbering in his mind. He needed to know how to help himself.

As teachers, we sometimes become "addicted" to approval. We tend to look toward others—parents, administrators, colleagues—to assess our teaching. Like the young man, we often can't step back and look at our teaching objectively. Usually we listen to others: "Tell me how I did. Did you like that lesson? Really? How could you think it was good?" We live in incredulity.

On the other hand, there are some (fewer and fewer, I hope) teachers who prefer to live the unexamined teaching life. Far from seeking approval, they keep their doors closed, refuse to participate in study groups, and often blame shortcomings on their students. But they are unlikely to read this book anyway, so I am not writing for them. I am most likely speaking to those who want to assess their teaching, but who work too hard without working smart. One way to work smart is to develop the broad vision to assess our own work objectively.

In this chapter, we will look at ways to live the "examined" teaching life. I hope we all learn to study our whole-class teaching and to self-assess every day. It is not the three-times-a-year formal evaluations or the informal drop-in visits by administrators that make us outstanding teachers. It is accepting nothing but the best from ourselves and knowing how to see the best (and the less than best) in our work. We'll look at two indicators of excellent teaching and one bit of advice.

- student work that mirrors what has been taught

- self-assessment in small and large steps: short-term and global views

- Angelillo's advice for a humane teaching life

Student Work That Mirrors What Has Been Taught

Perusal of student work provides a clear window into successful teaching. I have no doubt that there is a direct correlation between how well students read and write and the quality of the teaching they receive. And although I do not believe that statewide tests are the best indicators of how well students have been taught, good teaching should produce students who have little problem with statewide exams. So yes, we can use data from statewide exams, but we must also examine students' daily ongoing work. How much progress are students making in developing as good readers and writers? How are they learning to think flexibly and solve problems? How are they growing toward independence? How much of our teaching is consistently showing up in their work? Can we point to student work that has examples of lessons just taught, lessons taught weeks ago, and ongoing lessons about good thinking, reading and writing?

An old adage says that a parent's job is to put herself out of a job. And so it is with teachers. And we must be serious about it. We are successful when our students no longer need us.

To this end, I suggest that we examine student work as the litmus test of successful teaching. Within all student writing, there should be evidence of direct teaching, whether whole-class, small-group, or individual teaching. Furthermore, student work lets us evaluate which kind of teaching is our most effective as individuals. Do our conferences bring excellent results in terms of student follow-through and longevity? Or our small-group instruction? To what extent does our whole-class instruction show results in all students' work? If we find that, for example, small-group work is in general much more effective than whole-class instruction, this indicates a need to study whole-class instruction deeply. With the emphasis on differentiation, small-group work, and conferring—all of which are critically important to a complete instructional plan—I worry that some teachers believe their whole-class instruction is not that important. It is as if whole-class instruction is like a loosely woven sieve, and students who fall through the holes can be picked up in small groups and conferences. This is not healthy teaching. If too many students are falling through too many holes in whole-group instruction, it is time to do something about the instruction!

What does solid evidence of robust whole-class teaching look like? Examining student work, you want to see consistent and ongoing evidence of the following.

- immediate try-its of strategies that were taught during lessons, with evidence of students returning to strategies to try them again

- evidence of long-lasting lessons, that is, lessons on process and the writerly life, with expectations that shape student work over time

- students following through on work and using lessons cumulatively, that is, students noting in the margins strategies they learned, are trying again, are struggling to understand, and so on

- regular reading of student work to note where work from discrete lessons shows and/or where they have approximated or attempted it

- keeping records of when, and for which students, lessons become so automatic that they are independent

- noticing the amount of reteaching needed based on examination of student work

- noticing how the community is growing; supporting strategies for working and being together

Let's visit one teacher to study how he learns about his teaching from his students' work. Alex rereads his students' writing often. He hopes to learn about them as writers and readers, but also about what he should teach next. He tells me he does this reading with "two eyes"—one on student work and one on his own work. First he makes photocopies of all "final" drafts, knowing that we are never really done with writing. He returns the photocopies to students and asks them to indicate at least three to five places where they have deliberately used his teaching in their writing. (He also may ask them to mark places where they have used teaching from small groups or conferring.) Then he studies the papers to see what students have marked. Do they mark only his revision lessons? Are they mostly using strategies from this unit of study? Are they mostly using strategies from a previous unit of study? Are there skills he taught that seem to be automatic now? Is there something he needs to reteach because they've misunderstood or are not using it at all? Are they focusing on the grander things, like exciting beginnings, while ignoring the less theatrical, but just as important things, such as spelling or punctuation?

All this information takes time to collect, but Alex uses it carefully. He not only knows what his students have learned but what has "stuck" from previous lessons. He has a window into where his teaching is effective and where it is not. He has a sense of where to go next and how to make himself a better teacher (Figure 8–1a and b).

Self-Assessment in Small and Large Steps: Short-Term and Global Views

Assessment includes evaluating lessons from the current unit of study and previous units, the small steps and large steps of teaching. It makes sense to examine the immediate lessons and their effectiveness, but also to look back over the year—and not only at the end of the year. Just as we look back over student work in intervals—for example, quarterly, we can do this for our teaching.

It makes sense to look at each unit of study to assess how we've met goals, but also to do this cumulatively across the year. For example, if I examine how effective my teaching was in the first unit of study (usually Launching the Workshop), I may see lessons that I need to reteach during the second unit of study. Similarly, looking back over the first two units will give me information about what I need to teach in the third unit. This brings me to a quarterly assessment of my teaching in general, that is, the success of my teaching been in the first three units and using the information to plan a course from there. (See Figure 8–2.)

A chart such as the one in Figure 8–2 nudges us to look at the broad strokes of teaching. Studying individual lessons seems to be less difficult for us, as the lessons are easily contained in the content of one or a few days. Looking at long-term goals, such as "what I want students to know

Yankee Stadium

By

Leo Gonzalez

I went to Yankee Stadium with my dad for my birthday. He bought tickets in the nosebleed section. We ate hot dogs and cotton candy. Everyone wanted Derek Jeter to hit a home run. I was screaming, "Come on Derek." Alex Rodriguez is my favorite player, but I like Derek Jeter too. I was thinking that if Derek got a home run and I caught the ball it would be the best birthday present. Then Jason Giambi hit a home run! The ball came toward me! I was screaming! Then a man three rows behind me caught it. I was happy for him, but I felt bad I didn't catch it. The Yankees lost, so we went home. I had a good time with my dad on my birthday.

Figure 8–1a *Student marks evidence of using teacher's minilessons in his writing*

Yankee Stadium

By

Leo Gonzalez

I went to Yankee Stadium with my dad for my birthday. He bought tickets in the nosebleed section. We ate hot dogs and cotton candy. Everyone wanted Derek Jeter to hit a home run. I *Add dialogue* was screaming, "Come on Derek." Alex Rodriguez is my favorite *add thinking* player, but I like Derek Jeter too. I was thinking that if Derek got a home run and I caught the ball it would be the best birthday *Zoom in* present. Then Jason Giambi hit a home run! The ball came *Exciting punc* toward me! I was screaming! Then a man three rows behind me caught it. I was happy for him, but I felt bad I didn't catch it. The Yankees lost, so we went home. I had a good time with my dad on my birthday.

how you felt

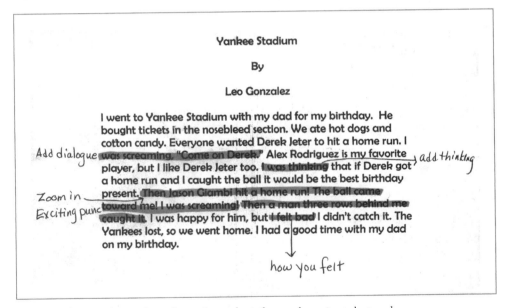

Figure 8–1b *Teacher marks evidence of several minilessons shown in student work*

Unit of Study + Date of Completion	Key Concepts	Effectiveness Evaluation: What Students Need	Long-Term Goals in This Unit	Possible Reteaching Plans
Launch of workshop (Sept. 20)	Community Keeping a notebook Quick notebook publish	Community weak 50% keeping notebook: independence; use of notebook to contain ideas and develop plans	Establish routines Get notebook going Teach writing process	*Community:* ongoing, reconsider read-aloud, room arrangement *Notebook:* Add a deep study to follow unit #2
Personal narrative (Oct. 28)	Beginning/middle/end Elements of story (plot, character) Use of the writing process	Notebook 60% Beg/mid/end good Revision refusals!	Write story prep for state test prompt Managing story elements: plot, character	Story elements: more read-alouds Teach revising in the notebook
Notebook study (Nov. 11)	Types of entries in notebook; notebook as tool for revision, planning, collecting, finding, and developing ideas; leading the writerly life	Improved to 85%	Use of notebook for thinking strategies	Small-group support for 20% struggling
Conventions study (Nov. 23)	Inquiry into punctuation	85% usage; some approximation	Punctuation as a code; symbols to create meaning	Plan one deeper study; grammar study
Quarterly assessment (by Nov. 30)	➤ Community beginning to gel; notebook usage improving; repeat personal narrative	➤ Personal narrative lessons too broad = repeat unit with specificity; work on independence	➤ Work on personal narrative in response to prompts before test	➤ Plot construction and character development; keep checking on notebooks

Figure 8–2 *Quarterly assessment of teaching*

after three months of teaching," is more challenging. But it forces us to be thoughtful, careful teachers. It forces us to manage our teaching better. It forces us to raise the stakes on ourselves, not just on the students. "How well have I taught in this quarter?" is more important than "How much did they get?"

Equally important is seeing when teaching is successful. Students learn from clear lessons, use what we've taught them in their reading and writing—or at least, make novice attempts to do so—and growth is evident. At these times, we need to congratulate ourselves. We need to celebrate! It makes good sense to record in your notebook *why* your teaching has been successful. Even success should prompt reflection, so that it can be repeated and enjoyed again. Of course, the nature of teaching does not guarantee the same lessons will succeed from one year to the next. But there is something about the teaching method that made it work, and that you can duplicate with some certainty of its effect.

- clarity and form

- appropriateness of content for the group

- use of text to support teaching

- use of modeling or demonstration

- thinking aloud about the content

- position of lesson within the unit, and unit within the year

- attention to qualities of good reading and writing

- modeling the transfer of skills from one context to another

- use of student assessment to plan teaching

Assessing Units of Study, Assessing Lessons

We all know there is too much to teach, so there can be no wasted lessons, no wasted days in any unit of study. Without a negative attitude, looking back over lessons in each unit can improve teaching dramatically. Within the fullness of school days, it is easy to lose hold of direction. Perhaps the class has come to a lull in energy—or the teacher has. Perhaps the class is at a struggling point before leaping to understand—or the teacher is struggling with this. Perhaps several students are having trying times at home that affect their work in class; or the teacher is experiencing difficulty himself. Assessment can clarify this, rather than drag us down into the morass of "I can't do this; this class doesn't get it; I've lost my gift" thinking. Assessment opens us to the light. We see how good our teaching really is, and we realize that we can make it better when we figure out how to "get over this hump." Knowing why we are hitting a wall is half the battle to breaking free of it.

At the end of units of study, ask yourself the following kinds of questions.

* Did I go off track and how did it happen?

* Did I lose energy for the unit and why?

* Did I get bogged down in one part of the process or the content and why?

* Do I need to find better mentor texts to use for my students?

* How did the whole-class teaching support small groups and conferring and visa versa?

* What would I do differently in terms of beginning or ending the unit?

Similar questions apply to minilessons, for in truth, humans can have "bad days," lost energy, or simply go off track in teaching lessons. Apart from these considerations, we can choose to examine a recent lesson or a long ago lesson with the objective eyes that come with the distance of time. Once again, following is a list of criteria to use while assessing yourself as a crafter of lessons.

* Did you work on form or art?

* Did you solely work on content?

* How did you use your own experience to build the lesson?

* What did you expect student to be able to do at the end of the lesson?

* Does your work show attention to your own reading and writing?

* How well do you know students' needs? The curriculum? Standards? Writing and reading workshop?

* How is your teaching elegant and exuberant?

Angelillo's Advice for a Humane Teaching Life

Take time to fall in love with teaching all over again. Never think of assessment as a negative part of our profession but rather as a way to live the examined teaching life, the way to get better and better at what we do. Use what you learn from assessment to make yourself better and to congratulate yourself on all you do well. Recognize that this is a journey. We are not the teachers who, once upon a time, collected 180 lessons and repeated them for twenty-five years! If those teachers ever existed, they are gone from our profession now. We work hard, every day. So learn to live in the moment with your class during each lesson and every minute of the day. Rest. Listen. Enjoy.

Summary

In order to improve our professional work, we must engage in equal parts of student assessment and assessment of our teaching. Looking back over lessons and units of study with a careful view gives us much information on how to revise teaching. It makes us wiser and smarter. It makes us more effective and generous. Most of all, it makes us better able to shape student learning, and in the long run, the shape of education in general, as we raise the bar on what is acceptable teaching.

For teachers to do

- Build in time for assessment.

- Work with other teachers to develop objective vision.

- Review lessons immediately and with the distance of time.

- Study lessons and units from various viewpoints.

- Examine student work as a litmus test of the effectiveness of teaching.

- Be good to yourself.

Teacher Study Groups: You Can Do This!

Once a week, a small group of inmates at a state prison meet together to study public speaking. Their hope is that at some point in their lives, they will be able to speak to others about their experiences. They hope to inspire others to a revised life and to uphold each other in the interim. They have grown a community that is strong, wise, and useful. I was invited to visit their study group this month. As a guest, I was able to observe and to notice how the nature of the study group dynamic changes and challenges people. I left surprised and filled with hope, thinking how wonderful it is to study together. It is affirming and safe, yet promotes expansive thinking, creativity, and risk taking,

Teacher study groups are powerful means for change. In fact, I hope and expect that most teachers will involve themselves in a study group at least once a year—for their own learning, to support the teaching community, and to build relationships that support and strengthen one another. I also believe there is another benefit to the study groups, one that I heard the inmates at their public speaking group say again and again: "You can do this!" Teacher study groups help us all feel that we can do this—we can assess and revise our teaching, no matter how far from our goal we feel at this moment. We help each other become wise teachers and our entire school community benefits in the long run.

To study whole-class teaching, teachers may take one of several approaches. They might choose to video- or audiotape their lessons asking for positive and constructive comments. Perhaps they will visit one another during preparation time to observe lessons. Some teachers tape their lessons and make transcripts of them for study. The important point is that study should help us to support each other and improve teaching, not create competition or criticism.

This chapter contains plans for several teacher study groups (and another bit of advice), though each "blueprint" should be taken as a suggestion, not a solid mandate. Each study group will find its own way, and the intention and purpose of the group may change as learning is uncovered. One thing that must not be compromised is the respect for each other in the group and the unflinching commitment to the work of becoming better teachers together.

Study Groups on Minilessons

This section contains details for organizing several possible study groups. As always, I believe in teacher choice. My intention is to suggest some ways to study whole-class teaching, but I hope and expect that teachers will invent their own. Study is an ongoing structure of the professional life. I know teachers will meet to study together many times over the year and over their careers.

Study groups often work best when teachers set a limit on the number of meetings. Given the many commitments teachers have, it is easier to commit to four weeks of meetings than to four months, though it is always possible to extend a study if participants so desire. Initially, start with short studies and invite all teachers, or all teachers at the grade level, to participate. Over time, the need for deeper study may become apparent. When this happens, schedule meetings over several months while being sensitive to time crunches during parent conference time or holidays. Make sure that the groups are poised to succeed. Ask an administrator to support the group. Food and coffee are always helpful, as are books or articles to read. Mostly, enjoy the time to be together, learning and laughing.

Study Group on Minilessons That Support Small-Group Teaching

Teachers often think of small-group and individual instruction as ways to close the holes in minilessons. There are times when small-group and individual instruction does offer additional support to students, though I prefer to think of these two teaching structures as times when we provide additional instruction tailored to student needs apart from the minilesson. Remember that we only can teach 180 or so minilessons, but there are many other skill, facts, and strategies we want students to know. Small-group and individual instruction is perfect for this. But weak minilessons have so many holes in them that we feel—justifiably—that we have to provide other teaching to plug up the holes. Small-group work might take a corner or branch of a minilesson and deepen it, but should not, in general, fix up the minilesson. Let's have no more sievelike teaching.

So imagine that a group of teachers wants to study how to make their minilessons robust and solid in order to free small-group and individual teaching to extend and challenge student learning. Teachers might set up intervisitations, audio- or videotape minilessons for review, make transcripts, consider careful planning, assess student work, and study small-group plans and conferring notes together. All this would provide a large amount of information. In addition, teachers might want to study together for several sessions. Four sessions of study might be organized as in Figure 9–1.

Study Group on Minilessons Across Units of Study

This study group will consider the kinds and content of minilessons that are not bound to any particular unit of study, but that might appear in all units of study with increasing difficulty. These lessons might include process, such as ways to revise, or content, such as knowledge of grammar.

Meeting #1: Teachers list the types of minilessons that occur across units of study and look for strands and connections. These might include conventions, grammar, revision strategies, use of the writers' or readers' notebooks, use of a mentor text, how to confer or work with a partner, and so on. Teachers examine their plans to ensure that these lessons are planned across units and agree to bring in examples of exact lessons to share with group members.

Meeting #2: Teachers study the minilessons they have brought for planning and effectiveness of accumulating knowledge, layering of information, and spiraling.

Meeting #3: Teachers study the progression of minilessons within each unit of study. What is the relationship to the content of the unit and how do the lessons support each other across units? For example, how does the use of punctuation in a feature article study inform what you will teach about punctuation in the following study?

Meeting #1: Teachers examine the relationship between minilessons and the small-group work they are doing. The study focuses on some of these questions:

- ❏ How do minilesson and other instructional structures flow from one to another?
- ❏ What is the symbiotic relationship of minilesson and differentiated instruction?
- ❏ Are they related at all?
- ❏ When this works—that is, the minilesson is a fountain from which the other structure flows—what characteristics of the teaching make it work?
- ❏ How might you replicate this?

Meeting #2: Teachers plan small-group work that flows from minilessons by studying two minilessons and sketching out the small-group work that would flow from them.

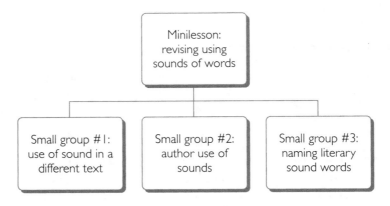

Meeting #3: Teachers study small-group work that jump-starts the next minilesson. This is small-group or individual teaching that precedes a minilesson to lay the groundwork for understanding a difficult or major concept. It may involve coaching some students so that the minilesson is actually the second time they hear the information.

Meeting #4: Assessment of one strand of minilesson and small-group work based on the scope of student understanding and student work to show how successful the teaching was.

Figure 9.1   *Plan for four-week teacher study group in minilessons and other instructional structures*

Meeting #4: Teachers assess the overall sense of the minilessons' fit into the units and with one another. They discuss the degree of randomness and how to make teaching deliberate but not rigid.

Other possible study groups

- using teacher writing to model during minilessons

- use of children's literature in whole-class teaching

- fluency and procedure in minilessons

- minilesson significance and importance

- deliberate and wise progression or order of minilessons in a unit of study

- minilessons that challenge students, that is, that are just on the edge of what students can do in order to stretch their learning

- minilessons that show thoughtful evidence of varied content and growth, not just of piling on new strategies and skills every day

You Can Do This!

I feared writing a book on whole-class teaching. I worried that the very writing of the book would make teaching seem so complicated and built on so many discrete parts that teachers would just throw up their hands and say, "We can't do this!" It would be tragic if that happens—I have comic nightmares of hundreds of teachers streaming from classrooms with tears streaming down their faces. . . .

But I wrote this to encourage and support you. I know you can do it, especially those of you who have chosen to read this book instead of the latest spy novel, literary tome, or magazine. I take your devotion to teaching seriously, and I thank you for it. I also know that our work is to become smarter, so the purpose of this book is to make us all smarter. Our students, our society, and our profession deserve no less. Here are some of my thoughts on how you can do this without becoming overwhelmed, exhausted, or discouraged!

Focus on the Important Things

Don't worry that you cannot teach students everything you believe they need to know. There will be other teachers, other grades, and other lessons for them to learn. For now, focus on the following points.

- Teach students something new every day, knowing you will only get to teach 180 lessons in reading and writing.

- Determine what all students should know and teach from there.

- Avoid cute activities, avoid your pet peeves (for example, they don't *all* have to read *Bridge to Terabithia* (Paterson 1996) or whatever your favorite book is; don't worry if they insist on wearing hats in school, and so on).

- Think about being smart and becoming smarter.

- Connect the threads of instruction for students so they see how everything fits together.

- See the bigger picture of how what you teach today will prepare students for later this year, next year, and years after that.

- Practice common sense.

Focus on Performance

To paraphrase The Bard, every classroom's a stage. Minilessons of every kind are performances. Teachers build a connection with their audience—their students—and they work that energy shamelessly. They use timing, humor, and an actor's skill to create lessons that are perfect mirrors of reality. The great teacher delivers a fine performance every day.

My actor friends tell me that when they prepare for roles, they know they must do research. But most of what they need is already inside their heads and hearts. The emotions they access, they gestures they need, and their understanding of human relationships are already there inside them. They use these to prepare their roles and to play to their audience. And they know that if their performances do not please audiences, the show will close.

Teachers, great actors that we are, also have what we need inside us. Like acting, ours is a wondrous art. And like actors, we may research in preparation for a unit of study or group of lessons. But when we work metacognitively, our curriculum grows from who we are and what we do.

We use our understanding of humanity, as well as of children and learning science, to help us craft lessons that provoke, inspire, and yes, entertain our audience. And heaven forbid that our audience is ever so unhappy (or unsuccessful) that the show must close! Every performance counts. So thinking about teaching as grand performance can help us imagine and prepare lessons.

* Realize that much of what you need to teach is already inside your head.

* Play your audience—draw energy from your students to give your best performance.

* Think about how you would feel or think or respond if you were in the audience, that is, the class.

* Rehearse, prepare, and plan.

* Trust your instincts.

* Use humor when you can.

* Don't be afraid to let students see you cry.

Focus on Rapture

Let us return to the moment when we each decided to be teachers. We all have stories to tell—often about the one teacher who inspired or believed in us. I recall suddenly knowing that the profession of teaching was a great gift, thanks to amazing teachers like Richard Peck, Jack McNeil, Rosemarie Laster, Miriam Balf, and a list of other magnificent teachers at my high school in Manhattan. I knew I had to teach. I was in love with teachers and teaching and writing and learning. Teaching could never be a "job." There was too much at stake! It was high theatre and mission work wrapped all together.

Every day, we awaken to a host of challenges. Teaching makes us very flexible, or regrettably for some, very rigid. Retool your mind to think of teaching as daily work with a sacred purpose. It changes everything. Rapture changes everything.

* Lose yourself in learning.

* Lose yourself in your students, with all their foibles.

* Fall in love with your own learning life and your metacognition.

- Fall in love with your students.

- Be surprised every day.

- Realize that the most unlovable student is in your class *to teach you something.*

- Live in the present.

- Trust yourself.

Take Care of Yourself

My dear friend and colleague Sarah Daunis once said to me, "If you don't take care of yourself, how can you take care of anyone else?" She said this to me at a point when I was doing too much, going to too many places, and trying to meet too many people's needs other than my own. I was "running on empty." I thank Sarah for her wisdom, kindness, and courage; she pointed out to me what I didn't see myself. I needed to take care of *me!*

This may seem like an odd statement in the context of studying and assessing teaching, but I think it belongs here. As teachers, we often drive ourselves to exhaustion. The demands of classroom, family, and school community can often overwhelm us, yet we tend to keep going. Most teachers I know are top-notch professionals, but their assessment of their work always consists of what they "should have or could have" done. More of our assessment must include what we are "approximating" or learning to do and applauding ourselves for living with the intention of revising our lives and our teaching.

So here are some thoughts about further study and assessment of the teaching life. Weigh your physical, emotional, spiritual, and professional needs. Be good to yourself. Build in time for exercise and refreshment. Eat well; take vitamins; read for pleasure. Treat yourself to an "artist's date" (Cameron 1992) once a week—that is, take yourself on a walk, to a museum, a bookstore, a coffee shop, a park bench. Even if it is only for fifteen minutes. You are an artist creating the most exquisite art—the glorious truth of magnificent teaching and learning. Learn to sit quietly. Learn to love yourself as much as you love your students and your work. Learn to listen. You deserve it. And your students deserve a teacher who is in command of her life and learning.

Summary

Study groups are powerful vehicles for teachers who want to grow strong together. The content of teaching improves by studying together, as does the teaching community itself. But study groups are more than "support groups." Study groups must be useful; new understandings and information must be generated from studying together. The whole group becomes more insightful in the process.

For teachers to do

- Join or initiate a study group.

- Watch your own teaching to figure out what you want to study next.

- Develop close relationships with colleagues where trust overcomes solitude and competition.

- Read professional books together; read and share children's books.

- Be good to yourself.

References

Anderson, C. 2000. *How's It Going?* Portsmouth, NH: Heinemann.

———. 2005. *Assessing Writers: A Practical Guide to Conferring with Students.* Portsmouth, NH: Heinemann.

Angelillo, J. 2002. *A Fresh Approach to Teaching Punctuation.* New York: Scholastic.

———. 2003. *Writing About Reading: From Book Talk to Literary Essay, Grades 3–8.* Portsmouth, NH: Heinemann.

Bomer, R., and K. Bomer. 2002. *For a Better World: Reading and Writing for Social Action.* Portsmouth, NH: Heinemann.

Calkins, L. M. 1994. *The Art of Teaching Writing.* 2nd ed. Portsmouth, NH: Heinemann.

———. 2000. *The Art of Teaching Reading.* New York: Allyn & Bacon.

Calkins, L., A. Hartman, and Z. White. 2005. *One to One: The Art of Conferring with Young Writers.* Portsmouth, NH: Heinemann.

Calkins, L. M., et al. 2003. *Units of Study for Primary Writing: A Yearlong Curriculum.* Portsmouth, NH: Heinemann FirstHand.

———. 2006. *Units of Study for Teaching Writing, Grades 3–5.* Portsmouth, NH: Heinemann FirstHand.

Cambourne, B., and J. Turbill. 1991. *Coping with Chaos.* Portsmouth, NH: Heinemann.

Cameron, J. 1992 *The Artist's Way.* New York: Jeremy Tarcher.

Carter, C., J. Bishop, J. Block, and S. Kravitz. 2006. *Keys to Effective Learning: Developing Powerful Habits of Mind.* 5th ed. Upper Saddle River, NJ: Prentice Hall.

Coles, R. 1991. *The Spiritual Lives of Children.* New York: Mariner.

Costa, A. 2001. *Developing Minds: A Resource Book for Teaching Thinking.* 3rd ed. Alexandria, VA: ASCD.

Costa, A., and B. Kallick. 2000. *Discovering and Exploring Habits of Mind.* Alexandria, VA: ASCD.

Flower, L. 1994. "Teachers as theory builders." In *Making Thinking Visible.* Edited by L. Flower, D. L. Wallace, L. Norris,, and R. E. Burnett. Urbana, IL: NCTE.

Fountas, I., and G. S. Pinnell. 1996. *Guided Reading: Good First Teaching for All Children.* Portsmouth, NH: Heinemann.

Fox, M. 2001. *Reading Magic: Why Reading Aloud to Our Children Will Change Their Lives Forever.* Orlando, FL: Harcourt.

Gee, J. 2004. *What Video Games Have to Teach Us About Learning and Literacy.* New York: Palgrave Macmillan.

Graves, D. 2003. *Writing: Teachers and Children at Work.* 20th anniversary ed. Portsmouth, NH: Heinemann.

Graves, D. H., and P. Kittle. 2005. *Inside Writing: How to Teach the Details of Craft.* Portsmouth, NH: Heinemann.

Hahn, M. L. 2002. *Reconsidering Read-Aloud.* York, ME: Stenhouse.

Hall, S. 2001. *Using Picture Storybooks to Teach Literary Devices.* Vol. 3. New York: Oryx.

Heitmen, J. 2004. *Teaching Writing to Older Readers Using Picture Books: Every Picture Tells a Story.* Worthington, OH: Linworth.

Hoyt, L. 2006. *Interactive Read Alouds, Grades K–1: Linking Standards, Fluency, and Comprehension.* Portsmouth, NH: Heinemann FirstHand.

Hunter, M. 1969. *Improved Instruction.* New York: Corwin Press.

Jensen, B. 2005. *Teaching with the Brain in Mind.* Alexandria, VA: ASCD.

Johnston, P. H. 2004. *Choice Words: How Our Language Affects Children's Learning.* York, ME: Stenhouse.

Kriete, R. 2002. *Morning Meeting.* 2nd ed. Turner Falls, MA: Northeast Foundation for Children.

Laminack, L. L., and R. M. Wadsworth. 2006a. *Learning Under the Influence of Language and Literature: Making the Most of Read-Alouds Across the Day.* Portsmouth, NH: Heinemann.

———. 2006b. *Reading Aloud Across the Curriculum: How to Build Bridges in Language Arts, Math, Science, and Social Studies.* Portsmouth, NH: Heinemann.

Meier, D. 1995 *The Power of Their Ideas: Lessons from America from a Small School in Harlem.* New York: Beacon.

Mermelstein, L. 2007. *Don't Forget to Share: The Crucial Last Step in the Writing Workshop.* Portsmouth, NH: Heinemann.

Murray, D. M. 2003. *A Writer Teaches Writing.* Portsmouth, NH: Heinemann.

O'Reilley, M. R. 1993. *The Peaceable Classroom.* Portsmouth, NH: Boynton/Cook.

———. 1998. *Radical Presence: Teaching as Contemplative Practice.* Portsmouth, NH: Boynton/Cook.

Palmer, P. J. 1998. *The Courage to Teach.* San Francisco: Jossey-Bass.

Pearson, M. B. 2005. *Big Ideas in Small Packages: Using Picture Books with Older Readers.* Worthington, OH: Linworth.

Perkins, D., A. L. Costa, and B. Kallick. 2000. *Activating and Engaging Habits of Mind.* Alexandria, VA: ASCD.

Paterson, K. 1996. *Bridge to Terabithia.* New York: HarperCollins.

Peterson, R. 1992. *Life in a Crowded Place: Making a Learning Community.* Portsmouth, NH: Heinemann.

Pullman, P. 2006. *The Golden Compass.* Anniverary ed. New York: Knopf.

Ray, K. W. 2000. *Wondrous Words.* Urbana, IL: NCTE.

———. 2002. *What You Know by Heart: How to Develop Curriculum for Your Writing Workshop.* Portsmouth, NH: Heinemann.

Ray, K., and L. L. Laminack. 2001. *Writing Workshop: Working Through the Hard Parts (and They're All Hard Parts).* Urbana, IL: NCTE.

Serafini, F., and Giordis, C. 2003. *Reading Aloud and Beyond: Fostering the Intellectual Life with Older Readers.* Portsmouth, NH: Heinemann.

Shaffer, D. W., K. R. Squire, R. Halverson, and J. P.Gee. 2005. "Video Games and the Future of Learning." *Phi Delta Kappan* 87 (2): 104–11.

Silver, H. F., R. W. Strong,, and M. J. Perini, 2000. *So Each May Learn: Integrating Learning Styles and Multiple Intelligences.* Alexandria, VA: ASCD.

Sizer, T. M. 1992. *Horace's School: Redesigning the American High School.* New York: Mariner.

Smith, F. 1987. *Joining the Literacy Club: Further Essays into Education.* Portsmouth, NH: Heinemann.

Tiedt, I. M. 2000. *Teaching with Picture Books in Middle School.* Newark, DE: IRA.

Tomlinson, C. A. 1999. *The Differentiated Classroom: Responding to the Needs of All Learners.* Alexandria, VA: ASCD.

Tyler, R. W. 1949. *Basic Principles of Curriculum and Instruction.* Chicago: University of Chicago Press.

Warren, M. R. 2005. "Communities and Schools: A New View of Urban Education Reform," *Harvard Educational Review* 75 (2): 133–73.

Wiggins, G., and J. McTighe. 2005. *Understanding by Design.* 2nd ed. Upper Saddle River, NJ: Prentice Hall.

Wilhelm, J. 2001. *Improving Comprehension with Think-Aloud Strategies: Modeling What Good Readers Do.* New York: Scholastic.

Wolfe, P. 2001. *Brain Matters: Translating Research into Classroom Practice.* Alexandria, VA: ASCD.

Zion, G. 1956. *Harry the Dirty Dog.* New York: HarperCollins.

Index

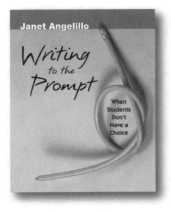

Writing to the Prompt
When Students Don't Have a Choice
Janet Angelillo

Writing to the Prompt demonstrates how to apply the best practices you already know to on-demand writing—without abandoning your workshop or topic choice. Janet Angelillo presents a unit of study that addresses timed-test situations and offers practical suggestions for ongoing assessment. You'll find humane teaching techniques that help students build facility with assigned topics and engage thoughtfully with third-party ideas.

2005 / 176pp / $19.50
978-0-325-00759-5 / 0-325-00759-4

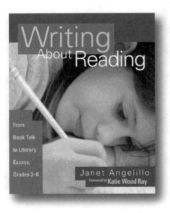

Writing About Reading
From Book Talk to Literary Essays, Grades 3–8
Janet Angelillo
Foreword by **Katie Wood Ray**

Want to know how to teach students to think and write powerfully about texts? Read this remarkable book now. You'll be glad you did.
— **Carl Anderson**, author of *How's It Going?*

Writing About Reading helps ensure that your students will be readers and writers long after they leave your classroom. Its ideas get kids enthused and empowered to use whatever they read as fuel for their writing lives.

2003 / 160pp / $18.50
978-0-325-00578-2 / 0-325-00578-8

www.heinemann.com

To place an order, **call 800.225.5800**, or **fax 877.231.6980.**